101 best campsites

by the **beach**

2014

alan rogers

Compiled by: **Alan Rogers Travel Ltd**

Designed by: **Vine Design Ltd**

© Alan Rogers Travel Ltd 2013

Published by: **Alan Rogers Travel Ltd,**
Spelmonden Old Oast, Goudhurst, Kent TN17 1HE
Tel: **01580 214000** www.**alanrogers**.com

British Library Cataloguing-in-Publication Data:
A catalogue record for this book is
available from the British Library.

ISBN 978-1-909057-29-6

Printed in Great Britain by
Stephens & George Print Group

Contents

Welcome to the Alan Rogers
'101' guides

The Alan Rogers guides have been helping campers and caravanners make informed decisions about their holiday destinations since 1968. Today, whether online or in print, Alan Rogers still provides an independent, impartial view, with detailed reports, on each campsite.

With so much unfiltered, unqualified information freely available, the Alan Rogers perspective is invaluable to make sure you make the right choice for your holiday.

What is the '101' series?

At Alan Rogers, we know that readers have many and diverse interests, hobbies and particular requirements. And we know that our guides, featuring a total of some 3,000 campsites, can provide a bewildering choice from which it can be difficult to produce a shortlist of possible holiday destinations.

The Alan Rogers 101 guides are devised as a means of presenting a realistic, digestible number of great campsites, featured because of their suitability to a given theme.

This book remains first and foremost an authoritative guide to excellent campsites which offer great seaside holidays.

101 Best campsites
by the beach

For many, a holiday is not a holiday unless a beach is involved. And none more so than camping holidays. The archetypal sun, sea and sand holiday is, for some, the ideal; for others it's dramatic blustery seascapes and clattering, pebble beaches; yet others prefer secluded little coves and rocky inlets.

Whichever you prefer, this guide features campsites that offer all kinds of beach. There are even wonderful campsites set beside magnificent lakes, complete with their own beach.

So whether you're planning an out-of-season, invigorating seaside break or the full, sandy, bucket and spade extravaganza this summer, read on. There are 101 campsites in this guide and, depending on what kind of beach you're looking for, you are sure to find your ideal holiday destination here.

Alan Rogers – in search
of 'the best'

Alan Rogers himself started off with the very specific aim of providing people with the necessary information to allow them to make an informed decision about their holiday destination. Today we still do that with a range of guides that now covers Europe's best campsites in 27 countries. We work with campsites all day, every day. We visit campsites for inspection purposes (or even just for pleasure!). We know campsites 'inside out'.

We know which campsites would suit active families; which are great for get-away-from-it-all couples; we know which campsites are planning super new pool complexes; which campsites offer a fantastic menu in their on-site restaurant; which campsites allow you to launch a small boat from their slipway; which campsites have a decent playing area for kicking a ball around; which campsites have flat, grassy pitches and which have solid hard standings.

We also know which are good for fishing, children, nature and outdoor activities; which are close to the beach; and which welcome dogs. These particular themes form our '101' series.

All Alan Rogers guides (and our website) are respected for their independent, impartial and honest assessment. The reviews are prose-based, without overuse of indecipherable icons and symbols.
Our simple aim is to help guide you to a campsite that best matches your requirements – often quite difficult in today's age of information overload.

What is
the best?

The criteria we use when inspecting and selecting sites are numerous, but the most important by far is the question of good quality. People want different things from their choice of campsite, so campsite 'styles' vary dramatically: from small peaceful campsites in the heart of the countryside, to 'all singing, all dancing' sites in popular seaside resorts.

The size of the site, whether it's part of a chain or privately owned, makes no difference in terms of it being required to meet our exacting standards in respect of its quality and it being 'fit for purpose'. In other words, irrespective of the size of the site, or the number of facilities it offers, we consider and evaluate the welcome, the pitches, the sanitary facilities, the cleanliness, the general maintenance and even the location.

Expert
opinions

We rely on our dedicated team of Site Assessors, all of whom are experienced campers, caravanners or motorcaravanners, to visit and recommend campsites. Each year they travel around Europe inspecting new campsites for Alan Rogers and re-inspecting the existing ones.

alanrogers.com/beach

When planning
your holiday...

A holiday should always be a relaxing affair, and a campsite-based holiday particularly so. Our aim is for you
to find the ideal campsite for your holiday, one that suits your requirements. All Alan Rogers guides provide
a wealth of information, including some details supplied by campsite owners themselves, and the
following points may help ensure that you plan a successful holiday.

Find out more

An Alan Rogers reference number (eg FR 12345) is given for each campsite and can be useful for finding more information and pictures online at www.alanrogers.com. Simply enter this number in the 'Campsite Search' field on the Home page.

Campsite descriptions

We aim to convey an idea of its general appearance, 'feel' and features, with details of pitch numbers, electricity, hardstandings etc.

Facilities

We list specific information on the site's facilities and amenities and, where available, the dates when these facilities are open (if not for the whole season). Much of this information is as supplied to us and may be subject to change. Should any particular activity or aspect of the campsite be important to you, it is always worth discussing with the campsite before you travel.

Swimming pools

Opening dates, any charges and levels of supervision are provided where we have been notified. In some countries (notably France) there is a regulation whereby Bermuda-style shorts may not be worn in swimming pools (for health and hygiene reasons). It is worth ensuring that you do take 'proper' swimming trunks with you.

Charges

Those given are the latest provided to us, usually 2013 prices, and should be viewed as a guide only.

Toilet blocks

Unless we comment otherwise, toilet blocks will be equipped with a reasonable number of British style WCs, washbasins and hot showers in cubicles. We also assume that there will be an identified chemical toilet disposal point, and that the campsite will provide water and waste water drainage points and bin areas. If not the case, we comment. We do mention certain features that some readers find important: washbasins in cubicles, facilities for babies, facilities for those with disabilities and motorcaravan service points.

Reservations

Necessary for high season (roughly mid-July to mid-August) in popular holiday areas (i.e. beach resorts). You can reserve many sites via our own Alan Rogers Travel Service or through other tour operators. Remember, many sites are closed all winter and you may struggle to get an answer.

Telephone numbers

All numbers assume that you are phoning from within the country in question. From the UK or Ireland, dial 00, then the country's prefix (e.g. France is 33), then the campsite number given, but dropping the first '0'.

Opening dates

Dates given are those provided to us and can alter before the start of the season. If you intend to visit shortly after a published opening date, or shortly before the closing date, it is wise to check that it will actually be open at the time required. Similarly some sites operate a restricted service during the low season, only opening some of their facilities (e.g. swimming pools) during the main season; where we know about this, and have the relevant dates, we indicate it – again if you are at all doubtful it is wise to check.

Accommodation

Over recent years, more and more campsites have added high quality mobile homes, chalets, lodges, gîtes and more. Where applicable we indicate what is available and you'll find details online.

Special Offers

Some campsites have taken the opportunity to highlight a special offer. This is arranged by them and for clarification please contact the campsite direct.

Life's
a beach

The lure of the coast, and the beach in particular, is a strong holiday motivation. Most people enjoy a holiday beside the sea and the many facets a beach has to offer holidaymakers of all ages. There are thousands of campsites across Europe, with many on or close to a great beach either on the coast or beside a shimmering lake. This guide features a shortlist of just 101, so read on and start dreaming…

Why
the beach...?

In the UK, it was not until the advent of the train in the late 19th century that the masses began to enjoy the benefits of a seaside holiday, fuelling growth of long piers. Later, from the 1920s, glamour became part of the mix, with the south of France attracting the likes of Hemingway and Picasso. An hotel was encouraged to stay open all summer and the Côte d'Azur has never looked back. Venerable fashionable resorts (Biarritz, La Baule) are still going strong; sandy expanses in the West Country are perennial favourites; the blustery Scandanavian beaches are atmospheric and unspoilt; and the vast sandy beaches of the Spanish Costas offer a special magic.

Finding the right
beach campsite

Sun, sea and sand...it sounds simple but finding the right balance can be difficult with a campsite beach holiday. Some people want to be right there in the action, right on the beach; others prefer a campsite that's set back from the hurly-burly, even if it means a short drive. Some simply want miles of sand, with or without the crowds, others search for secluded rocky coves, perhaps seeking out that perfect spot beneath a shady pine.

You will find campsites with majestic sweeping sea views, campsites which run regular shuttle buses to and from the beach – especially handy when parking is at a premium; some campsites have their very own private stretch of beach and this may vary between sand, shingle, craggy rocks and dunes.

Quality Beaches

What makes a good beach? Which is the best beach in the area? Which beach is best for children? These are all valid questions but everyone will have their own opinion.

Blue Flag

Blue Flag is a prestigious international award scheme for beaches which acts as a guarantee of quality. Awarded annually to over 3,450 beaches and marinas in 41 countries, the award of a Blue Flag is based on compliance with 32 criteria covering the aspects of environmental education and information, water quality, environmental management, safety and services.

Children
on beaches

Family memories are made of long sunny days at the beach: splashing in the shallows, sandcastles, sandy sandwiches, buckets of crabs.

A good family beach, especially for young children, will have clean sand (ideally of the kind that makes good sandcastles), gently sloping down to the sea. Hopefully the sea at low tide is not a mile away, allowing toddlers to paddle while remaining close by (although a lovely wide beach does allow plenty of room for games and kite flying). And of course an ice cream vendor can usually bring a few squeals of pleasure!

Activities
for children

Some larger beaches often have activities specially for children, usually in high season – these could range from playgrounds or boating lakes right up to paid-for clubs with organised activities all day. And of course, in the UK the traditional donkey ride still exists!

For the younger ones

- Dig a channel to the sea
- Make a dam
- Bury dad in the sand
- Go beach combing for the most interesting "find"
- Build a boat or a car in the sand big enough to sit in – always makes an amusing snap for the album!

Ping Pong Ball Race

Dig a series of sloping channels wide enough (and smooth enough) to take a ping pong ball. Place ping pong balls at the start line and then race each other, blowing the ball down the channel to the finish line.

Beach Minigolf

Create your own minigolf course in the sand. Players take turns with a plastic golf club and ball – or whatever implement you can find.

Frisbee

A perennial favourite. Set up some targets in the sand and see who can get closest, or arrange plastic bottles in the sand and try to knock them over.

Go prepared and keep a bat and ball in the car – there's always a demand for French cricket, boules, badminton and kite flying.

Water Fun

Many lakeside campsites, especially in Austria, Hungary and Slovenia, have pedaloes, rowing boats and floating pontoons, as well as on-shore activities.

Activities
on the beach

With a bracing breeze, a good boost of ozone and loads of space, a beach always seems to invite activity.

It could be a fairly sedate activity like beach combing, throwing the odd stick for the dog or flying a kite.

Fishing too is popular, available all year, and for free.

More strenuous and physical activities might include power kiting and sand yachting
– popular on the long, wide, flat sandy beaches.

Surfing

By definition, good surfing beaches will involve turbulent waters so try and surf where a lifeguard is present and not on your own. Only surf within your own ability and experience, making sure you are surfing in safe locations.

Kayaking

A great way to spend time on the water but don't take this too lightly – you should be familiar with the necessary kit and precautions. Check the weather, wind and tides, wear a buoyancy aid and ideally paddle in a group, telling someone back on land where you are going. Make sure you can get back on board your kayak should you capsize.

Staying safe
at the beach

Beaches are a fun environment but it pays to be aware of potential dangers. In particular, keep an eye on tides – incoming tides can quickly trap people in coves or under cliffs. If unsure, check with a lifeguard. The RNLI beach safety tips are applicable anywhere.

Top Tips

• Always swim at a lifeguarded beach

• Swim between the red and yellow flags *(UK)*

• Never swim alone

• Never use inflatables in strong winds or rough seas

• If you get into trouble, wave and call for help

• If you see someone else in trouble, tell a lifeguard or call emergency services

• Take note of warnings and notices

Enjoy...!

Whether you're an 'old hand' or are contemplating your first trip, a regular reader of our Guides or a new 'convert', we wish you well in your travels and hope we have been able to help in some way. We are, of course, also out and about ourselves, visiting sites, talking to owners and readers, and generally checking on standards and new developments. We hope to bump into you!

Wishing you thoroughly enjoyable camping and caravanning in 2014 – favoured by good weather of course!

The Alan Rogers Team

Further
information

www.goodbeachguide.co.uk – *Website of the Marine Conservation Society*

www.blueflag.org – *The international organisation responsible for awarding the Blue Flag for beaches (and marinas)*

www.onbeach.nl – *Dutch website with information and lists of European beaches*

www.maplage.fr – *French website with extensive information on French beaches*

www.esplaya.com – *English-language website on the many beaches in Spain*

www.italyheaven.co.uk – *English-language website on the beaches of Italy*

www.kustgids.nl and www.holland.com – *Respectively, a Dutch and an English-language website on the beaches of the Netherlands*

Facilities: Five excellent large toilet blocks with electronic sliding glass doors (resident cleaners 07.00-21.00). British style toilets but no seats, controllable hot showers and washbasins in cabins. Excellent facilities for youngsters, babies and disabled campers. Laundry facilities. Motorcaravan services. Extensive supermarket, boutique and other shops. Large bar with terrace. Large restaurant. New takeaway and terrace in 2012. Ice cream parlour. Beach bar in main season. Disco club. Swimming pools. Playgrounds. Tennis. Archery. Minigolf. Sailing/windsurfing school and other watersports. Programme of sports, games, excursions and entertainment, partly in English (15/6-31/8). Exchange facilities. ATM. Safety deposit. Internet café. WiFi over site (charged). Dogs taken in one section. Torches required in some areas. Off site: Resort of L'Escala 5 km. Riding and boat launching 5 km. Water park 10 km. Golf 30 km.

Open: 18 May - 14 September.

Directions: L'Escala is northeast of Girona on coast between Palamós and Roses. From A7/E15 autostrada take exit 5 towards L'Escala on GI623. Turn north 2 km. before L'Escala towards Sant Marti d'Ampúrias. Site signed.

GPS: 42.16098, 3.107774

Charges guide

Per unit incl. 2 persons and electricity	€ 22,50 - € 68,00
extra person	€ 3,50 - € 6,00
child (3-10 yrs)	€ 3,00 - € 3,50
dog	€ 3,20 - € 5,00

Spain – Sant Pere Pescador

Camping Las Dunas

Ctra San Marti-Sant Pere, E-17470 Sant Pere Pescador (Girona)
t: 972 521 717   e: info@campinglasdunas.com
alanrogers.com/ES80400   www.campinglasdunas.com

Accommodation: ☑ Pitch ☑ Mobile home/chalet ○ Hotel/B&B ○ Apartment

Las Dunas is an extremely large, impressive and well organised resort-style site with many on-site activities and an ongoing programme of improvements. It has direct access to a superb sandy beach that stretches along the site for nearly a kilometre with a windsurfing school and beach bar. There is also a much used, huge swimming pool, plus a large double pool for children. Las Dunas is very large, with 1,700 individual hedged pitches (1,500 for touring units) of around 100 sq.m. laid out on flat ground in long, regular parallel rows. All have electricity (6/10A) and 180 also have water and drainage. Shade is available in some parts of the site. Much effort has gone into planting palms and new trees here and the results are very attractive. A disco club is close by in a soundproofed building (although people returning from this during the night can be a problem for pitches in the central area of the site). With free, quality entertainment of all types in season and positive security arrangements, this is a great site for families with teenagers. A popular site for British rallies. A member of Leading Campings group.

You might like to know

Adjacent to the site is the 3 km. golden sandy beach of Sant Pere Pescador. It is a unique landscape bordered by soft dunes.

☑ Beach on site
○ Beach within 1 km
☑ Sandy beach
○ Blue Flag quality
○ Lifeguard *(high season)*
○ Sun lounger and/or deckchair hire
☑ Watersports *(e.g. sailing or windsurfing)*
○ Snacks and drinks
○ Sunshades/sunbeds
○ Dogs allowed *(on the beach)*

Camping la Ballena Alegre

Ctra Sant Marti d'Empuries s/n, E-17470 Sant Pere Pescador (Girona)
t: 972 520 302 e: info@ballena-alegre.com
alanrogers.com/ES80600 www.ballena-alegre.com

Accommodation: ☑ Pitch ☑ Mobile home/chalet ○ Hotel/B&B ○ Apartment

Facilities: Seven well maintained toilet blocks are of a very high standard. Facilities for children, babies and disabled visitors. Launderette. Motorcaravan services. Gas supplies. Comprehensive range of restaurants, snack bars and takeaways, including a pizzeria/trattoria, arroceria, a pub, a self-service restaurant and a beach bar in high season. Swimming pool complex (four pools including one for children). Jacuzzi. Tennis. Watersports centre. Fitness centre. Bicycle hire. Playgrounds. Soundproofed disco. Dancing twice weekly and organised activities, sports, entertainment, etc. ATM. Dogs only allowed in one zone. Internet and WiFi (charged). Torches useful in beach areas. Off site: Go-karting nearby with bus service. Fishing 300 m. Riding 2 km.

Open: 17 May - 21 September.

Directions: From A7 Figueres-Girona autopista take exit 5 to L'Escala GI623 for 18.5 km. At roundabout take sign to Sant Marti d'Empúries and follow site signs.

GPS: 42.15323, 3.11248

Charges guide

Per unit incl. 2 persons and electricity	€ 26,50 - € 57,00
extra person	€ 4,00 - € 5,00
child (3-10 yrs)	€ 2,80 - € 3,30
dog	€ 2,30 - € 4,80

Discount of 10% on pitch charge for pensioners all season.
No credit cards.

La Ballena Alegre is a spacious site with almost 2 km. of frontage directly onto an excellent beach of soft golden sand. They claim that none of the 966 touring pitches is more than 100 m. from the beach. The grass pitches are individually numbered, many separated by hedges, and there is a choice of size (up to 120 sq.m). Electrical connections (5/10A) are available in all areas and there are 670 fully serviced pitches. There are several bungalow areas within the site with their own small pools and play areas, and some have shared jacuzzis. There are restaurant and bar areas beside the terraced pool complex. For those who wish to drink and snack late there is a pub open until 03.00. The soundproofed disco is popular with youngsters. Plenty of entertainment and activities are offered, including a watersports centre, with sub-aqua, windsurfing and kite-surfing, where equipment can be hired and lessons taken. The site has won Spanish tourist board awards and the owners are keen to promote an ecological approach through recycling, use of solar energy and the design of new buildings. This is a great site for families.

You might like to know

The site has a well stocked beach shop so that you can make the most of the 1,800 m. long sandy beach.

- ☑ Beach on site
- ○ Beach within 1 km
- ☑ Sandy beach
- ○ Blue Flag quality
- ○ Lifeguard (high season)
- ○ Sun lounger and/or deckchair hire
- ☑ Watersports (e.g. sailing or windsurfing)
- ○ Snacks and drinks
- ○ Sunshades/sunbeds
- ○ Dogs allowed (on the beach)

Facilities: Four very well equipped toilet blocks are immaculately maintained and well spaced around the site. Baby baths. Laundry facilities. Motorcaravan services. Gas supplies. Fridge hire. Large supermarket. Restaurant/bar, swimming and paddling pools (all season). Three play areas. Small botanical garden. Entertainment for children and adults (July/Aug). Sports courts. Sailing, water skiing, windsurfing, diving, canoe hire. Fishing. Bicycle hire. Excursions. ATM. Internet access and WiFi over part of site (charged). Torches required in some areas. Doctor service in high season. Off site: Tossa de Mar 3 km. Bicycle hire 3 km.

Open: 14 April - 28 September.

Directions: Leave the AP7/E15 at exit 7 to the C65 Sant Feliu road and then take C35 southeast to the GI681 to Tossa de Mar. Site is signed off the GI682 Lloret-Tossa road at km. 18,9, 3 km. from Tossa. Route avoids difficult coastal road.

GPS: 41.71292, 2.906465

Charges guide

Per unit incl. 2 persons and electricity (6A)	€ 30,70 - € 52,00
extra person	€ 6,35 - € 9,25
child (4-12 yrs)	€ 3,65 - € 5,75
dog	€ 5,10 - € 5,45

Camping Cala Llevadó

Ctra GI-682 de Tossa a Lloret km. 18,9, E-17320 Tossa de Mar (Girona)
t: 972 340 314 e: info@calallevado.com
alanrogers.com/ES82000 www.calallevado.com

Accommodation: ☑ Pitch ☑ Mobile home/chalet ○ Hotel/B&B ○ Apartment

Cala Llevado is a beautifully situated and quiet (although popular), cliff-side site, enjoying fine views of the sea and coast below. It is shaped around a wooded valley with steep access roads and terracing. High up on the site with a superb aspect is the attractive restaurant/bar with a large terrace overlooking the pleasant swimming pool directly below. There are terraced, flat touring pitches (with 10/16A electricity) on the upper levels of the two slopes, with a great many individual pitches for tents scattered around the site. Many of these pitches have fantastic settings and views. The site is unsuitable for campers with disabilities. In some areas cars may be required to park separately. There are 45 tour operator pitches, 34 bungalows and six new glamping cabins. One beach is for all manner of watersports within a buoyed area and there is a sub-aqua diving school. There are three other pleasant coves, including a naturist area, that can be reached by climbing down on foot (with care!). The site is peacefully situated but only five minutes away from the busy resort of Tossa.

You might like to know

There are some beautiful beaches within easy reach, in one of the most scenic parts of the Costa Brava.

- ☑ Beach on site
- ○ Beach within 1 km
- ☑ Sandy beach
- ○ Blue Flag quality
- ○ Lifeguard *(high season)*
- ○ Sun lounger and/or deckchair hire
- ☑ Watersports *(e.g. sailing or windsurfing)*
- ☑ Snacks and drinks
- ○ Sunshades/sunbeds
- ○ Dogs allowed *(on the beach)*

Facilities: Very modern, fully equipped, heated sanitary blocks are kept spotlessly clean by omnipresent cleaners. Baby baths and brilliant facilities for children. Washing machines and dryers. Shop, extensive modern complex of restaurants, bars and takeaways (all open all season). Infinity pool (June onwards, lifeguard). Pool bar. Play areas. Kayak hire. Bicycle hire. Organised activities for children in high season. Diving school. Sports centre. WiFi over site (charged). ATM. Private access to beach. Off site: Road train to town centre from outside site. Cala Montgó beach 100 m. GR92 coastal path 50 m. Fishing 150 m. Riding 2 km. Golf 10 km.

Open: 11 March - 20 October.

Directions: From north on A7 take exit 3 to N11, then C31 and GI 623 signed l'Escala. From south take exit 5 from A7 signed l'Escala. Site is clearly marked from town.

GPS: 42.11051, 3.16542

Charges guide

Per unit incl. 2 persons
and electricity € 24,30 - € 51,25

extra person € 3,50 - € 6,90

child (3-10 yrs) € 2,45 - € 4,75

dog € 2,55 - € 4,35

No credit cards.

Spain – L'Escala

Camping Illa Mateua

Avenida de Montgó 260, E-17130 L'Escala (Girona)
t: 972 770 200 e: info@campingillamateua.com
alanrogers.com/ES80740 www.campingillamateua.com

Accommodation: ☑ Pitch ☑ Mobile home/chalet ○ Hotel/B&B ○ Apartment

If you prefer a quieter site, out of the very busy resort of L'Escala, then Illa Mateua is an excellent option. This large, family run site has a dynamic owner Marti, who speaks excellent English. The site is divided by the beach access road and has its own private accesses to the contrasting beaches – one a rocky cove and the other gentle, sandy and sloping. There are 350 pitches across both parts of the site, all with 6A electricity, some on sloping ground, although the pitches in the second part are flat. Established pine trees provide shade for most places with more coverage on the western side. A new purpose-built diving centre and club opened on the site in 2013, offering a comprehensive programme of training. There are two swimming pools, the largest an 'infinity' pool enjoying an idyllic and most unusual setting on the top of a cliff overlooking the Bay of Roses. The second pool in the bar, restaurant and terrace area is scheduled for redevelopment in 2014. A CCTV system monitors the pools and general security. There are bungalows to rent, including one for disabled visitors, which is normally booked well in advance.

You might like to know

The beach has hammocks and pedaloes for hire, and there is good access for disabled visitors.

☑ Beach on site
○ Beach within 1 km
☑ Sandy beach
☑ Blue Flag quality
○ Lifeguard *(high season)*
○ Sun lounger and/or deckchair hire
☑ Watersports *(e.g. sailing or windsurfing)*
○ Snacks and drinks
☑ Sunshades/sunbeds
○ Dogs allowed *(on the beach)*

Camping Resort Sanguli Salou

Passeig Miramar-Plaça Venus, Apdo 123, E-43840 Salou (Tarragona)
t: 977 381 641 e: mail@sanguli.es
alanrogers.com/ES84800 www.sanguli.es

Accommodation: ☑ Pitch ☑ Mobile home/chalet ○ Hotel/B&B ○ Apartment

Camping Resort Sanguli Salou is a superb site boasting excellent pools and entertainment. Owned, developed and managed by a local Spanish family, it has something for all the family with everything open when the site is open. There are 1,090 pitches of varying sizes (70-100 sq.m) and all have electricity (7.5-10A). Mobile homes occupy 58 pitches and there are fully equipped bungalows on 147. A wonderful selection of trees, palms and shrubs provides natural shade and an ideal space for children to play. The good sandy beach is little more than 50 metres across the coast road and a small railway crossing. Although large, Sanguli has a pleasant, open feel and maintains a quality family atmosphere due to the efforts of the efficient staff. There are three very attractive themed pools which include water slides and elephants. Evening shows are presented in the magnificent amphitheatre. The site's restaurant serves Mediterranean cuisine. This is a large, professional site providing something for all the family, but still capable of providing peace and quiet.

You might like to know

Activities on the beach include windsurfing, sailing, waterskiing, pedaloes and 800 m. from here, sea fishing. The attractive seafront promenade will take you into the centre of Salou.

- ○ Beach on site
- ☑ Beach within 1 km
- ☑ Sandy beach
- ☑ Blue Flag quality
- ☑ Lifeguard *(high season)*
- ☑ Sun lounger and/or deckchair hire
- ☑ Watersports *(e.g. sailing or windsurfing)*
- ☑ Snacks and drinks
- ☑ Sunshades/sunbeds
- ○ Dogs allowed *(on the beach)*

Facilities: The six sanitary blocks are constantly cleaned and are always exceptional, including many individual cabins with en-suite facilities. Improvements are made each year. Some blocks have excellent facilities for babies. Launderette with service. Motorcaravan services. Car wash (charged). Gas supplies. Snack bars. Indoor and outdoor restaurants with takeaway. Swimming pools. Fitness centre. Sports complex. Fitness room (charged). Playgrounds including adventure play area. Miniclub. Minigolf. Tennis. Football. Volleyball. Amphitheatre. Cinema. Communal barbecue. Multiple Internet options including WiFi (free). Security bracelets. Well equipped medical centre. Off site: Activities on the beach, 50 m. Bus at gate. Bicycle hire 100 m. Fishing 200 m. Riding 3 km. Port Aventura 4 km. Aquopolis and golf 5 km.

Open: 15 March - 3 November.

Directions: On west side of Salou 1 km. from the centre, site is well signed from the coast road to Cambrils and from the other town approaches.
GPS: 41.075, 1.116

Charges guide

Per unit incl. 2 persons and electricity	€ 29,00 - € 78,00
extra person	€ 7,00
child (4-12 yrs)	€ 5,00

Reductions outside high season for longer stays. Special long stay offers for senior citizens.

Facilities: Five very well maintained, fully equipped, toilet blocks include units for disabled visitors and babies and new facilities for children. Washing machines. Gas supplies. Large supermarket, bakery and souvenir shops at entrance, open to public. Full restaurant. Takeaway. Bar with large terrace where entertainment is held daily. Beach bar. Coffee bar and ice cream bar. Pizzeria. Open-roof cinema with permanent seating for 520. 3 TV lounges. Soundproofed disco. Swimming pools (two heated). Solarium. Sauna. Two large jacuzzis. Seawater jacuzzi and Turkish sauna. Sports areas. Tennis. Squash. Language school (Spanish). Minigolf. Sub-aqua diving (first dive free). Bicycle hire. Fishing. Windsurfing school. Sailboards and pedaloes for hire. Playground, crèche and Happy Camp. Fridge hire. Library. Hairdresser. Business centre. WiFi. Car repair and car wash (pressure wash). No animals permitted. No jet skis accepted. Off site: Buses on N340 close to site. Port Aventura. Beach fishing. Riding 3 km. Golf 4 km.

Open: 15 March - 31 October.

Directions: Entrance is off main N340 road by 1136 km. marker, 30 km. from Tarragona towards Valencia. From motorway take Cambrils exit and turn west on N340.

GPS: 41.03707, 0.97478

Charges guide

Per unit incl. 2 persons and electricity	€ 20,30 - € 66,55
extra person	€ 3,35 - € 9,90
child (0-10 yrs)	no charge - € 7,85

Discounts in low season for longer stays.

Spain – Montroig

Camping La Torre del Sol

Ctra N340 km. 1136, E-43300 Montroig (Tarragona)
t: 977 810 486 e: info@latorredelsol.com
alanrogers.com/ES85400 www.latorredelsol.com

Accommodation: ☑ Pitch ☑ Mobile home/chalet ☑ Hotel/B&B ○ Apartment

A pleasant banana tree-lined approach road gives way to avenues of palms as you arrive at Torre del Sol. This is a very large, well designed site occupying a good position in the south of Catalunya with direct access to the soft sand beach. The site is exceptionally well maintained by a large workforce. There is good shade on a high proportion of the 1,500 individual, numbered pitches (700 for touring). All have electricity and are mostly of about 90 sq.m. Strong features are 800 m. of clean beachfront, three attractive pools with two jacuzzis in the bar and restaurant area. A new seawater jacuzzi and Turkish sauna were opened in 2012. The cinema doubles as a theatre to stage shows all season. The complex of three pools, thoughtfully laid out with grass sunbathing areas and palms, has a lifeguard. There is wireless Internet access throughout the site. There is usually space for odd nights but for good places between 10/7-16/8 it is best to reserve (only taken for a stay of seven nights or more). There is a separate area where the activities team will take your children to camp overnight in the Indian reservation. Occasional train noise on some pitches.

You might like to know

The campsite has its own private beach, which is cleaned daily and hosts regular games and entertainment.

- ☑ Beach on site
- ○ Beach within 1 km
- ☑ Sandy beach
- ○ Blue Flag quality
- ☑ Lifeguard *(high season)*
- ○ Sun lounger and/or deckchair hire
- ○ Watersports *(e.g. sailing or windsurfing)*
- ☑ Snacks and drinks
- ○ Sunshades/sunbeds
- ○ Dogs allowed *(on the beach)*

Camping Playa Joyel

Playa de Ris, E-39180 Noja (Cantabria)
t: 942 630 081   e: playajoyel@telefonica.net
alanrogers.com/ES90000   www.playajoyel.com

Accommodation: ☑ Pitch   ☑ Mobile home/chalet   ○ Hotel/B&B   ○ Apartment

This very attractive holiday and touring site is some 40 kilometres from Santander and 80 kilometres from Bilbao. It is a busy, high quality, comprehensively equipped site by a superb beach providing 1,000 well shaded, marked and numbered pitches with 6A electricity available. These include 80 large pitches of 100 sq.m. Some 250 pitches are occupied by tour operators and seasonal units. This well managed site has a lot to offer for family holidays with much going on in high season when it gets crowded. The swimming pool complex (with lifeguard) is free to campers and the superb beaches are cleaned daily mid-June to mid-September. Two beach exits lead to the main beach where there are some undertows, or if you turn left you will find a reasonably placid estuary. An unusual feature here is the nature park within the site boundary which has a selection of animals to see. This overlooks a protected area of marsh where European birds spend the winter.

Facilities: Six excellent, spacious and fully equipped toilet blocks include baby baths. Large laundry. Motorcaravan services. Gas supplies. Freezer service. Supermarket (all season). General shop. Kiosk. Restaurant and takeaway (1/7-31/8). Bar and snacks (all season). Swimming pools, bathing caps compulsory (20/5-15/9). Entertainment organised with a soundproofed pub/disco (July/Aug). Gym park. Tennis. Playground. Riding. Fishing. Nature animal park. Hairdresser (July/Aug). Medical centre. Torches necessary in some areas. Animals are not accepted. WiFi (charged). Off site: Bicycle hire and large sports complex with multiple facilities including an indoor pool 1 km. Sailing and boat launching 10 km. Riding and golf 20 km.

Open: 30 March - 30 September.

Directions: From A8 (Bilbao-Santander) take km. 185 exit and N634 towards Beranga. Almost immediately turn right on CA147 to Noja. In 10 km. turn left at multiple campsite signs and go through town. At beach follow signs to site.
GPS: 43.48948, -3.53700

Charges guide

Per unit incl. 2 persons and electricity	€ 28,20 - € 47,40
extra person	€ 4,40 - € 6,70
child (3-9 yrs)	€ 3,10 - € 5,00

Low season discounts.

You might like to know

The fine sandy beach, which is excellent for surfing, is cleaned daily. At low tide there are warm pools for splashing in and rock pools with small fish and crabs.

- ☑ Beach on site
- ○ Beach within 1 km
- ☑ Sandy beach
- ○ Blue Flag quality
- ○ Lifeguard *(high season)*
- ○ Sun lounger and/or deckchair hire
- ☑ Watersports *(e.g. sailing or windsurfing)*
- ○ Snacks and drinks
- ○ Sunshades/sunbeds
- ○ Dogs allowed *(on the beach)*

Facilities: The clean, well maintained toilet block is modern with British style toilets, open style washbasins and hot showers, plus beach showers. Facilities for disabled visitors and babies. Laundry facilities. Motorcaravan services. Supermarket, bar with satellite TV (1/6-30/9). Restaurant and takeaway (1/6-15/9). Bicycle hire. Entertainment in high season. Charcoal barbecues are permitted. Off site: Beach and fishing 100 m. Bus service 800 m. Kayak excursions. Birdwatching.

Open: All year.

Directions: From the north, turn off the main coast road (N13-E50) just after camping sign at end of embankment alongside estuary, 1.5 km. south of ferry. From the south on N13 turn left at Hotel Faz de Minho at start of estuary and follow for 1 km. through woods to site.

GPS: 41.86635, -8.85844

Charges guide

Per unit incl. 2 persons and electricity	€ 15,00 - € 31,30
extra person	€ 3,40 - € 5,70
child (5-10 yrs)	€ 1,70 - € 2,90
dog	€ 1,00 - € 2,00

Off season discounts (up to 70%).

Orbitur Camping Caminha

EN13 km. 90, Mata do Camarido, P-4910-180 Caminha (Viana do Costelo)
t: 258 921 295 e: infocaminha@orbitur.pt
alanrogers.com/PO8010 www.orbitur.pt

Accommodation: ☑ Pitch ☑ Mobile home/chalet ○ Hotel/B&B ○ Apartment

In northern Portugal, close to the Spanish border, this pleasant site is just 200 m. from the beach. It has an attractive and peaceful setting in woods alongside the river estuary that marks the border with Spain and on the edge of the little town of Caminha. Of the 262 pitches, just 25 are available for touring with electricity (5/15A Europlug), the remainder are occupied by permanent units and chalets for rent. The site is shaded by tall pines with other small trees planted to mark large sandy pitches. The main site road is surfaced but elsewhere take care not to get trapped in soft sand. Pitching and parking can be haphazard. Static units are grouped together on one side of the site. Water points, electrical supply and lighting are good. With a pleasant, open feel about the setting, fishing and swimming are possible in the estuary, and from the rather open, sandy beach.

You might like to know

The site is close to the Spanish border and just 200 m. from a beautiful sandy beach, ideal for swimming and fishing.

○ Beach on site
☑ Beach within 1 km
☑ Sandy beach
☑ Blue Flag quality
○ Lifeguard *(high season)*
○ Sun lounger and/or deckchair hire
☑ Watersports *(e.g. sailing or windsurfing)*
○ Snacks and drinks
☑ Sunshades/sunbeds
○ Dogs allowed *(on the beach)*

Facilities: Four clean toilet blocks have mainly British style toilets (some with bidets), some washbasins with hot water. Hot showers are mostly in one unisex block. Laundry. Motorcaravan services. Gas supplies. Supermarket (1/6-15/9). Large restaurant and bar with terrace (1/6-15/9). Swimming pools (1/6-30/9). Satellite TV. Games room. Playground. Tennis. Free WiFi over part of site. Off site: Bus service 100 m. Beach 500 m. Fishing 1 km.

Open: All year.

Directions: Site is 9 km. west of Marinha Grande, on the right as you enter São Pedro de Moel.

GPS: 39.75883, -9.02229

Charges guide

Per person € 3,80 - € 6,40	
child (5-10 yrs) € 1,90 - € 3,20	
pitch € 8,50 - € 14,30	
electricity € 3,50	

Off season discounts (up to 70%).

Orbitur Camping São Pedro de Moel

Rua Volta do Sete, P-2430 São Pedro de Moel (Leiria)
t: 244 599 168   e: infospedro@orbitur.pt
alanrogers.com/PO8100 www.orbitur.pt

Accommodation: ☑ Pitch   ☑ Mobile home/chalet   ○ Hotel/B&B   ○ Apartment

This quiet and very attractive site is situated under tall pines, on the edge of the rather select small resort of São Pedro de Moel. This is a shady site which can be crowded in July and August. The 525 pitches are in blocks and unmarked (cars may be parked separately) with 404 electrical connections. A few pitches are used for permanent units. Although there are areas of soft sand, there should be no problem in finding a firm place. The large restaurant and bar are modern as is the superb swimming pool, paddling pool and flume (there is a lifeguard). The attractive, sandy beach is a 600 m. walk downhill from the site (you can take the car, although parking may be difficult in the town) and is sheltered from the wind by low cliffs.

You might like to know

The sheltered beach is only 600 m. away from the campsite.

○ Beach on site
☑ Beach within 1 km
☑ Sandy beach
○ Blue Flag quality
○ Lifeguard *(high season)*
○ Sun lounger and/or deckchair hire
☑ Watersports *(e.g. sailing or windsurfing)*
☑ Snacks and drinks
☑ Sunshades/sunbeds
○ Dogs allowed *(on the beach)*

Facilities: Four toilet blocks are well located around the site. Two have been refurbished, two are new and contain modern facilities for disabled campers. Hot water throughout. Facilities for children. Dog shower. Washing machines. Shop. Gas supplies. Restaurant/bar. Swimming pool (Mar-Oct) with two terraces and new jacuzzi. Aqua gymnastics. New wellness facility (2012). Bicycle hire. Entertainment in high season on the bar terrace. Two children's playgrounds. Adult art workshops. Miniclub (5-12 yrs) in season. Boules. Archery. Sports field. Cable TV. Internet. WiFi on payment. Bungalows to rent. Off site: Bus to Lagos and other towns from Praia da Luz village 1.5 km. Fishing and beach 2 km. Golf 3 km. Sailing and boat launching 5 km. Riding 7 km.

Open: All year.

Directions: Take exit 1 from the N125 Lagos-Vila do Bispo. The impressive entrance is 3 km. on the right.

GPS: 37.10111, -8.73278

Charges guide

Per unit incl. 2 persons and electricity	€ 17,00 - € 33,00
extra person	€ 4,00 - € 6,50
child (3-10 yrs)	no charge - € 3,50
dog	€ 5,00

Portugal – Lagos

Yelloh! Village Turiscampo

EN125, Espiche, Luz, P-8600 Lagos (Faro)
t: 282 789 265 e: info@turiscampo.com
alanrogers.com/PO8202 www.yellohvillage.co.uk/camping/turiscampo

Accommodation: ☑ Pitch ☑ Mobile home/chalet ○ Hotel/B&B ○ Apartment

This good quality site has been thoughtfully refurbished and updated since it was purchased by the friendly Coll family, who are known to us from their previous Spanish site. The site provides 206 pitches (70 sq.m) for touring units, mainly in rows of terraces, all with electricity (6/10A) and some with shade. Thirty-six deluxe pitches have water and waste water. The upper areas of the site are mainly used for bungalow accommodation (and are generally separate from the touring areas). A new, elevated, Californian-style pool and a children's pool have been constructed. The supporting structure is a clever water cascade and surround, with a large sun lounger area on astroturf. One side of the pool area is open to the road. The restaurant/bar has been tastefully refurbished and Roberto and his staff are delighted to use their excellent English, providing good fare at most reasonable prices. The restaurant has two patios, one for live entertainment and discos in season, and the other for dining out. This is a very good site for families and for 'snowbirds' to over-winter.

You might like to know

The campsite is 4 km. from Lagos and a little further is Portimão, both with superb sandy beaches.

○ Beach on site
○ Beach within 1 km
☑ Sandy beach
○ Blue Flag quality
○ Lifeguard *(high season)*
○ Sun lounger and/or deckchair hire
☑ Watersports *(e.g. sailing or windsurfing)*
☑ Snacks and drinks
○ Sunshades/sunbeds
○ Dogs allowed *(on the beach)*

Facilities: Five toilet blocks provide British and Turkish style toilets, washbasins with cold water, hot showers plus facilities for disabled visitors. Washing machines. Motorcaravan services. Gas supplies. Supermarket. Self-service restaurant and separate takeaway (June-Sept). Swimming pools (23/3-30/9). General room with bar and satellite TV. Free WiFi over part of site. Tennis. Open-air disco (high season). Off site: Bus from gate to Faro. Beach 600 m. Fishing and bicycle hire (summer) 1 km. Golf 4 km.

Open: All year.

Directions: Turn off N125 for village of Almancil. In the village take road south to Quarteira. Site is on the left 1 km. after large, official town welcome sign.

GPS: 37.06666, -8.08333

Charges guide

Per person € 6,50	
child (5-10 yrs) € 3,30	
pitch € 22,70	
electricity € 3,50	

Off season discounts (up to 70%).

Portugal – Quarteira

Orbitur Camping Quarteira

Estrada da Fonte Santa, avenida Sá Cameiro, P-8125-618 Quarteira (Faro)
t: 289 302 826   e: infoquarteira@orbitur.pt
alanrogers.com/PO8220 www.orbitur.pt

Accommodation: ☑ Pitch ☑ Mobile home/chalet ○ Hotel/B&B ○ Apartment

This is a large, busy, attractive site on undulating ground with some terracing, taking 795 units. On the outskirts of the popular Algarve resort of Quarteira, it is 600 m. from a sandy beach which stretches for a kilometre to the town centre. Many of the unmarked pitches have shade from tall trees and there are a few small individual pitches of 50 sq.m. with electricity and water. There are 659 electrical connections. Like others along this coast, the site encourages long winter stays. There is a large restaurant and supermarket which have a separate entrance for local trade. The swimming pools (free for campers) are excellent, featuring pools for adults (with a large flume) and children (with fountains).

You might like to know

The city of Faro is a bus ride away – the bus leaves from outside the campsite gate; alternatively, visit Almancil and the São Lourenço Church.

○ Beach on site
☑ Beach within 1 km
☑ Sandy beach
○ Blue Flag quality
○ Lifeguard *(high season)*
☑ Sun lounger and/or deckchair hire
☑ Watersports *(e.g. sailing or windsurfing)*
☑ Snacks and drinks
☑ Sunshades/sunbeds
○ Dogs allowed *(on the beach)*

Facilities

Facilities: Five excellent, refurbished toilet blocks are well designed and very clean. Free hot water in all facilities, mostly British style WCs and excellent facilities for disabled visitors. Baby showers and baths. Washing machines. Motorcaravan services. Large supermarket, small general shop (all season). Large bar and restaurant with takeaway (all season). Swimming pools (15/5-15/9). Tennis. Fishing. Bicycle hire. Playground. Full entertainment programme in season. Internet access. Dogs are restricted to specific areas and not allowed on the beach. Off site: Golf 500 m. Riding 10 km.

Open: 21 April - 24 September.

Directions: Site is 4 km. east of Grado on road to Monfalcone. Venice-Trieste motorway exit at Reipuglia-Monfalcone, first roundabout take second exit, direction airport and follow Grado signs for 13 km. Site is on the left opposite a golf course.

GPS: 45.69649, 13.45595

Charges guide

Per unit incl. 2 persons
and electricity € 19,90 - € 46,10

extra person € 5,70 - € 10,70

child (3-16 yrs) € 3,60 - € 9,70

dog € 3,20 - € 6,20

Less 10% for longer stays out of season.

Italy – Grado

Villaggio Turistico Europa

Via Monfalcone 12, I-34073 Grado (Friuli - Venézia Giúlia)
t: 043 180 877 e: info@villaggioeuropa.com
alanrogers.com/IT60050 www.villaggioeuropa.com

Accommodation: ☑ Pitch ☑ Mobile home/chalet ○ Hotel/B&B ○ Apartment

This large, flat, good quality site is beside the sea and has 500 pitches, with 400 for touring units. They are all neat, clean and marked, most with shade and 6/10A electricity, 300 are fully serviced. The terrain is undulating and sandy in the areas nearer the sea, where cars have to be left in parking places. An impressive, large new aquatic park covers 1,500 sq.m. with two slides (100 m. and 60 m. long) and many other features. With many shallow areas it is very popular with children and there are lifeguards. A new pool bar is an attractive feature. There is direct access to the beach. The water recedes up to 200 m. from the beach, but leaves a natural paddling pool which is enjoyed by children when it is hot. A narrow wooden jetty gives access to deeper water. This is a neat, well managed site which is probably the best in the area.

You might like to know

Various catamaran excursions to nearby nature reserves depart from the Villaggio Europa pier.

- ☑ Beach on site
- ○ Beach within 1 km
- ☑ Sandy beach
- ○ Blue Flag quality
- ○ Lifeguard *(high season)*
- ☑ Sun lounger and/or deckchair hire
- ☑ Watersports *(e.g. sailing or windsurfing)*
- ○ Snacks and drinks
- ☑ Sunshades/sunbeds
- ○ Dogs allowed *(on the beach)*

Facilities: Fourteen well kept, fully equipped toilet blocks which open and close progressively during the season; 11 have facilities for disabled visitors. Launderette. Motorcaravan service points. Gas supplies. Comprehensive shopping areas set around a pleasant piazza (all open till late). Eight restaurants each with a different style plus 11 pleasant and lively bars. Impressive aqua parks (all season). Tennis. Riding. Minigolf. Skating. Bicycle hire. Archery. Two fitness tracks in 4 ha. natural park with play area and supervised play. Golf academy. Diving centre and school. Windsurf school in season. Boat excursions. Recreational events. Hairdressers. Internet cafés. ATM. Dogs are not accepted. WiFi over site (charged). Off site: Boat launching 3.5 km. Aqualandia (special rates).

Open: 24 April - 29 September (with all services).

Directions: From Venice-Trieste autostrada leave at exit for airport or Quarto d'Altino and follow signs first for Jesolo and then Punta Sabbioni, and site will be seen just after Cavallino on the left.

GPS: 45.467883, 12.530367

Charges guide

Per unit incl. 2 persons
and electricity € 28,70 - € 53,80

with services € 29,20 - € 68,50

extra person € 6,60 - € 11,80

child (1-11 yrs acc. to age)
€ 3,70 - € 9,70

Italy – Cavallino-Treporti

Camping Union Lido Vacanze

Via Fausta 258, I-30013 Cavallino-Treporti (Veneto)
t: 041 257 5111 e: info@unionlido.com
alanrogers.com/IT60200 www.unionlido.com

Accommodation: ☑ Pitch ☑ Mobile home/chalet ☑ Hotel/B&B ☑ Apartment

This amazing site is very large, offering everything a camper could wish for. It is extremely well organised and it has been said to set the standard that others follow. It lies right beside the sea with direct access to a 1.2 km. long, broad sandy beach which shelves very gradually and provides very safe bathing (there are lifeguards). The site itself is regularly laid out with parallel access roads under a covering of poplars, pine and other trees providing good shade. There are 2,200 pitches for touring units, all with 6/10A electricity and 1,749 also have water and drainage. Because of the size of the site, there is an internal road train and amenities are repeated across the site (cycling is not permitted and cars are parked away from the pitches). You really would not need to leave this site – everything is here, including a sophisticated wellness centre. Overnight parking is provided outside the gate with electricity, toilets and showers for those arriving after 21.00.

You might like to know

One of Europe's largest sites, looking straight out to the Adriatic with a long private beach (1,200 metres), Union Lido is a top quality holiday centre with a wide range of amenities.

- ☑ Beach on site
- ○ Beach within 1 km
- ☑ Sandy beach
- ☑ Blue Flag quality
- ☑ Lifeguard *(high season)*
- ☑ Sun lounger and/or deckchair hire
- ☑ Watersports *(e.g. sailing or windsurfing)*
- ☑ Snacks and drinks
- ☑ Sunshades/sunbeds
- ○ Dogs allowed *(on the beach)*

Facilities: Five sanitary blocks, with all the usual facilities including free, controllable showers, washbasins in cabins, facilities for disabled visitors, children's area and baby room. Motorcaravan service point. Bars, restaurants, pizzeria and ice cream parlour. Supermarket and shopping centre plus first aid centre and a Murano glass shop. Swimming pools, paddling pools and hydromassage centre. Aquapark with waterslides (charged). Fitness centre. Solarium. Gym. Bowls. Tennis. Playground. Windsurfing school. Diving school. Games room. Entertainment and activity programme. Children's club. Excursions. Mobile homes and chalets for rent. Off site: Venice and Caorle.

Open: 21 April – 24 September.

Directions: From A4 motorway (Venice-Trieste) take exit to Ste Stino di Livenza and follow signs to Caorle joining the P59. Site is signed from Caorle on the continuation of this road to Porto Santa Margherita.

GPS: 45.56709, 12.7943

Charges guide

Per unit incl. 2 persons and electricity	€ 13,00 - € 45,00
extra person	€ 3,00 - € 10,00
child (3-6 yrs)	no charge - € 6,50

Italy – Caorle

Camping San Francesco

Porto Santa Margherita, I-30020 Caorle (Veneto)
t: 042 129 82 e: info@villaggiosfrancesco.com
alanrogers.com/IT60110 www.villaggiosfrancesco.com

Accommodation: ☑ Pitch ☑ Mobile home/chalet ○ Hotel/B&B ○ Apartment

Camping San Francesco is a large, beachside site in a quiet location close to the coastal town of Caorle (Little Venice), known for its connection with Ernest Hemingway. Although there are over 600 mobile homes to rent, 370 level, grassy pitches are reserved for tourers. They are close to the beach, shaded, and all have electricity (10A) and fresh and waste water connections. The site has every facility for a comfortable holiday, with swimming pools, an attractive aquapark (extra charge), a good beach for swimming, a large supermarket etc. However, some touring in the area from the site and a trip to Venice are also worthwhile. The large, well organised reception is supplemented by a separate information office at the flower-decked entrance to the site. At the end of the entrance road, near the fountain, are some shops and an ice cream parlour. The shop selling Murano glass will be of particular interest, especially if you are not already acquainted with the colourful products from the islands just north of Venice.

You might like to know

There are two beaches, only one of which is dog friendly. This has a designated water space and playground for dogs.

- ☑ Beach on site
- ○ Beach within 1 km
- ☑ Sandy beach
- ○ Blue Flag quality
- ○ Lifeguard *(high season)*
- ☑ Sun lounger and/or deckchair hire
- ☑ Watersports *(e.g. sailing or windsurfing)*
- ○ Snacks and drinks
- ☑ Sunshades/sunbeds
- ☑ Dogs allowed *(on the beach)*

Facilities: Three superb toilet blocks are kept pristine and have hot water throughout. Facilities for disabled visitors. Washing machines. Large supermarket and shopping centre, bars, restaurants, cafés and pizzeria (all season; takeaway service 15/5-30/9). Excellent pool complex with slide and spa centre (30/3-25/9). Tennis. Games room. Playground. Children's clubs. Entertainment programme. WiFi (charged). Direct beach access. Windsurf and pedalo hire. Mobile homes, chalets and 14 eco apartments for rent. Off site: ATM 500 m. Riding and boat launching 1 km. Golf and fishing 4 km. Walking and cycling trails. Excursions to Venice.

Open: 28 March - 30 September.

Directions: From A4 autostrada (approaching from Milan) take Mestre exit and follow signs initially for Venice airport and then Jesolo. From Jesolo, follow signs to Cavallino from where site is well signed.

GPS: 45.47380, 12.54903

Charges guide

Per unit incl. 2 persons and electricity	€ 20,00 - € 50,40
extra person	€ 5,00 - € 10,90
child (2-5 yrs)	€ 3,35 - € 9,90
dog	€ 2,65 - € 5,90

Italy – Cavallino-Treporti

Camping Village Europa

Via Fausta 332, I-30013 Cavallino-Treporti (Veneto)
t: 041 968 069 e: info@campingeuropa.com
alanrogers.com/IT60410 www.campingeuropa.com

Accommodation: ☑ Pitch ☑ Mobile home/chalet ○ Hotel/B&B ☑ Apartment

Europa is a large site in a great position with direct access to a fine, sandy, Blue Flag beach with lifeguards. There are 500 touring pitches, 450 of which have 8A electricity, water, drainage and satellite TV connections. There is a separate area for campers with dogs, and some smaller pitches are available for those with tents. The site is kept beautifully clean and neat and there is an impressive array of restaurants, bars, shops and leisure amenities. These are cleverly laid out along an avenue and include a jeweller's, a doctor's surgery, Internet services and much more. Leisure facilities are arranged around the site. The touring area is surprisingly peaceful for a site of this size. A professional team provides entertainment and regular themed summer events. Some restaurant tables have pleasant sea views. Venice is easily accessible by bus and then ferry from Punta Sabbioni.

You might like to know

Europa Camping Village has direct access to a vast, wide beach of very fine sand. Cleaned daily, it features natural dunes and is ideal for young children.

- ☑ Beach on site
- ○ Beach within 1 km
- ☑ Sandy beach
- ☑ Blue Flag quality
- ☑ Lifeguard *(high season)*
- ☑ Sun lounger and/or deckchair hire
- ☑ Watersports *(e.g. sailing or windsurfing)*
- ☑ Snacks and drinks
- ○ Sunshades/sunbeds
- ○ Dogs allowed *(on the beach)*

Facilities: Nine modern toilet blocks are maintained to a high standard with good hot showers and a reasonable proportion of British style toilets. Good provision for disabled visitors. Washing machines and dryers. Range of shops. Several bars, restaurants and takeaways. Swimming pool complex with slides and flumes. Several play areas. Tennis. Surfboard and catamaran hire. Wide range of organised entertainment. WiFi in the Bar Blu and Bar Rosa, Piazza Europa and the telephone office. Church. Special area and facilities for dog owners (also beach area). Off site: Fishing 1 km. Riding 7 km. Golf 10 km.

Open: 12 April - 30 September.

Directions: From A4 motorway, take Jesolo exit. After Jesolo continue towards Punta Sabbioni. Site is clearly signed to the left towards the end of this road, close to the Venice ferries.
GPS: 45.43750, 12.43805

Charges guide

Per unit incl. 2 persons and electricity	€ 21,40 - € 47,70
extra person	€ 4,60 - € 10,50
child or senior (2-5 and over 60)	€ 3,80 - € 8,50
dog	€ 1,30 - € 4,20

Italy – Punta Sabbioni

Camping Marina di Venezia

Via Montello 6, I-30013 Punta Sabbioni (Veneto)
t: 041 530 2511   e: camping@marinadivenezia.it
alanrogers.com/IT60450   www.marinadivenezia.it

Accommodation: ☑ Pitch   ☑ Mobile home/chalet   ○ Hotel/B&B   ○ Apartment

This is a very large site (2,915 pitches) with much the same atmosphere as many other large sites along this appealing stretch of coastline. Marina di Venezia, however, has the advantage of being within walking distance of the ferry to Venice. It will appeal in particular to those who enjoy an extensive range of entertainment and activities and a lively atmosphere. Individual pitches are marked out on sandy or grassy ground; most are separated by trees or hedges. They are of average size for the region (around 80 sq.m) and all are equipped with electricity and water. The site's excellent sandy beach is one of the widest along this stretch of coast and has five pleasant beach bars. The 15,000 sq.m. wide, multi-level AquaMarina Park has exceptional facilities - a feature pool for children with slides and a cascade, an Olympic size pool with massage jets, a lagoon with disability access, and a wave pool with a beach. This is a well run site with committed staff.

You might like to know

The coast features natural sand dunes, golden sand and safe bathing. There are well trained and equipped lifeguards, and deckchairs and beach umbrellas for hire. Sporting activities include beach volleyball, beach football, bowls, surfing, kite-surfing, canoeing and sailing.

- ☑ Beach on site
- ○ Beach within 1 km
- ☑ Sandy beach
- ☑ Blue Flag quality
- ☑ Lifeguard *(high season)*
- ☑ Sun lounger and/or deckchair hire
- ☑ Watersports *(e.g. sailing or windsurfing)*
- ☑ Snacks and drinks
- ☑ Sunshades/sunbeds
- ○ Dogs allowed *(on the beach)*

Facilities: Four modern sanitary blocks provide hot water for showers, washbasins and washing. Mostly British style toilets. Single locked unit for disabled visitors. Laundry facilities. Freezer. Motorcaravan service point. Good shop. Bar/restaurant and takeaway. Outdoor swimming pool. Play area. Miniclub and entertainment (high season). Fishing. Satellite TV and cartoon cinema. Internet access (free in low season). Kayak hire. Tennis. Torches useful. Bicycle hire. Off site: Boat launching 500 m. Bicycle track 1.5 km. Town with all the usual facilities and ATM 2 km. Riding 3 km. Golf 7 km.

Open: 5 April - 12 October.

Directions: From A22 Verona-Bolzano road take turn for Trento on S47 to Levico Terme where campsite is very well signed.

GPS: 46.00799, 11.28454

Charges guide

Per unit incl. 2 persons and electricity	€ 9,50 - € 38,00
extra person	€ 3,00 - € 14,25
child (3-11 yrs)	no charge - € 6,50
dog	no charge - € 5,00

Italy – Levico Terme

Camping Lago di Levico

Localitá Pleina, I-38056 Levico Terme (Trentino - Alto Adige)
t: 046 170 6491   e: info@campinglevico.com
alanrogers.com/IT62290   www.campinglevico.com

Accommodation: ☑ Pitch ☑ Mobile home/chalet ○ Hotel/B&B ○ Apartment

Camping Lago di Levico, by a pretty lakeside in the mountains, is the merger of two popular sites, Camping Levico and Camping Jolly. Brothers Andrea and Geno Antoniolli are making great improvements; already, there is an impressive new reception and further developments of the lakeside and swimming areas are planned. The lakeside pitches are quite special. There are 430 mostly grassy and shaded pitches (70-120 sq.m) with 6A electricity, 150 also have water and drainage and 12 have private facilities. Staff are welcoming and fluent in English. The swimming pool complex is popular, as is the summer family entertainment. There is a small supermarket on site and it is a short distance to the local village. The restaurant, bar, pizzeria and takeaway are open all season. The beautiful grass shores of the lake are ideal for sunbathing and the crystal clear water is ideal for enjoying (non-motorised) water activities. This is a site where the natural beauty of an Italian lake can be enjoyed without being overwhelmed by commercial tourism.

You might like to know

There is a large, private beach, but the clear, shallow waters of the lake offer opportunities for swimming, fishing, canoeing, and boating. Canoes and pedaloes can be hired from reception.

☑ Beach on site
○ Beach within 1 km
○ Sandy beach
☑ Blue Flag quality
☑ Lifeguard *(high season)*
○ Sun lounger and/or deckchair hire
○ Watersports *(e.g. sailing or windsurfing)*
☑ Snacks and drinks
☑ Sunshades/sunbeds
☑ Dogs allowed *(on the beach)*

Facilities: Two very clean and modern sanitary blocks near reception have British and Turkish style WCs and hot water throughout. Laundry. Motorcaravan services. Combined restaurant/bar/pizzeria/takeaway and shop. A swimming pool and paddling pool (1/4-31/10) and private beach. Tennis. Volleyball. Excellent play area. Wood-burning stove and barbecue. Fishing. Diving. Entertainment for children and adults in high season. Excursions. Bicycle hire. WiFi over site. Off site: Supermarket 200 m. Bus 200 m. Aquapark 500 m. Riding and golf 2 km. Ancient town of Albenga (2,000 years old) 3 km. Parachuting school 10 km. Local markets.

Open: 20 March - October, 6 December - 10 January.

Directions: From the A10 between Imperia and Savona, take Albenga exit. Follow signs Ceriale/Savona and Aquapark Caravelle (which is 500 m. from site) and then site signs. Site is just south of Savona.

GPS: 44.08165, 8.21763

Charges guide

Per unit incl. up to 3 persons (over 2 yrs) and electricity € 23,00 - € 51,00

extra person € 6,50 - € 11,00

dog € 3,00 - € 5,00

Discounts for stays in excess of 7 days.

Italy – Ceriale

Camping Baciccia

Via Torino 19, I-17023 Ceriale (Ligúria)
t: 018 299 0743 e: info@campingbaciccia.it
alanrogers.com/IT64030 www.campingbaciccia.it

Accommodation: ☑ Pitch ☑ Mobile home/chalet ○ Hotel/B&B ○ Apartment

This friendly, family run site is a popular holiday destination. Baciccia was the nickname of the present owner's grandfather who grew fruit trees and tomatoes on the site. Tall eucalyptus trees shade the 106 flat touring pitches. Laura and Mauro work tirelessly to ensure that you enjoy your stay here and we have watched the growth of a very effective campsite over the years. An informal restaurant, overlooking the swimming pool and sports area, is cheerfully and efficiently run by Flavio and Pamela who serve delightful seasonal Italian dishes. The pool has a giant elephant slide which is always busy. There is a free shuttle to the site's private beach and the town has the usual seaside attractions. This site will suit campers looking for a family atmosphere with none of the brashness of large seaside sites. If you have forgotten anything by way of camping equipment just ask and the family will probably be able to lend it to you.

You might like to know

Baciccia is just 500 m. from the free beach, and 1.5 km. from the private beach (free shuttle bus).

○ Beach on site
☑ Beach within 1 km
☑ Sandy beach
☑ Blue Flag quality
☑ Lifeguard *(high season)*
☑ Sun lounger and/or deckchair hire
☑ Watersports *(e.g. sailing or windsurfing)*
☑ Snacks and drinks
☑ Sunshades/sunbeds
○ Dogs allowed *(on the beach)*

Facilities: Three sanitary blocks. One is newly renovated with private bathrooms, and facilities for children and disabled visitors. The two older blocks have mixed Turkish/British style toilets. Washing machine. Motorcaravan service point (extra charge). Shop, restaurant and snack bar/takeaway (10/5-30/9). Live music concerts. Dog beach. Miniclub and entertainment in high season. Tennis. Water aerobics. Sailing. Sub-aqua diving. Windsurfing school. Riding. Torches essential. Bicycle hire. WiFi over site (charged). Communal barbecues. Off site: Riding 500 m.

Open: 20 April - 12 October.

Directions: Site is in southeast corner of Sardinia in the north of the Costa Rei. From coast road SS125 or the SP97 at km. 6, take the turn to Villaggio Capo Ferrato. Site is well signed from here.
GPS: 39.2923, 9.5987

Charges guide

Per unit incl. 2 persons and electricity	€ 22,50 - € 50,50
extra person	€ 5,00 - € 14,00
child (1-9 yrs acc. to age)	€ 2,00 - € 10,00
dog	€ 3,00 - € 6,00

Italy – Muravera

Tiliguerta Camping Village

S.P. 97 km. 6 - Loc. Capo Ferrato, I-09043 Muravera (Sardinia)
t: 070 991 437   e: info@tiliguerta.com
alanrogers.com/IT69750   www.tiliguerta.com

Accommodation: ☑ Pitch ☑ Mobile home/chalet ☑ Hotel/B&B ○ Apartment

This family site situated at Capo Ferrato has changed its owners, name and direction (2011). The new owners have made many improvements, all of them in sympathy with the environment. The 186 reasonably sized pitches are on sand and have 3A electricity. Some have shade and views of the superb, fine beach and sea beyond. The traditional site buildings are centrally located and contain a good quality restaurant using only fresh ingredients. This has a charming ambience with its high arched ceilings. Shaded terraces allow comfortable viewing of the ambitious entertainment programme. Cars must be parked away from pitches. The staff are cheerful and English is spoken. Consideration is given to the environment at every turn. There are numerous activities on offer – basketball, beach volleyball, riding and watersports, and in high season yoga, tai-chi, Pilates and dancing are possible. We believe Tiliguerta is becoming a good quality, environmentally friendly site.

You might like to know

Tiliguerta is directly beside the sea. It is the perfect place to enjoy one of Sardinia's most beautiful beaches, Costa Rei. Other beaches include the wild, dark sand coves of Feraxi and Colostrai, and the white sand beaches of Porto Pirastu, San Pietro, Cala Sinzias, Cala Pira and Timi Ama.

☑ Beach on site
☑ Beach within 1 km
☑ Sandy beach
○ Blue Flag quality
☑ Lifeguard (high season)
☑ Sun lounger and/or deckchair hire
☑ Watersports (e.g. sailing or windsurfing)
☑ Snacks and drinks
☑ Sunshades/sunbeds
☑ Dogs allowed (on the beach)

Facilities: Two sanitary blocks include toilets, washbasins and free hot showers. No facilities for disabled visitors. Washing machine and dryer. Baby room. Motorcaravan service point. Bar. Restaurant. Pizzeria. Well stocked shop. TV room. Bicycle hire. Tennis. Football and basketball pitch. New, comprehensive, well shaded children's play area. Entertainment (high season). WiFi (charged). Dogs are not accepted in July/Aug. Bungalows to rent. Off site: Sailing and boat launching 200 m. ATM in village. Riding 3 km. Golf 20 km. Costa Rei, Castiadas, Muravera, Villasimius.

Open: 1 April - 2 November.

Directions: Camping Capo Ferrato is in the southeast of Sardinia and can be reached by using the coast road towards Villasimius (SP17 or SS 125) then take the Costa Rei signs and the site is well signed on the southern edge of the village of Costa Rei. The site is in Costa Rei (Via delle Ginestre) and not on the promontory of Capo Ferrato.

GPS: 39.24297, 9.56941

Charges guide

Per unit incl. 2 persons and electricity	€ 22,20 - € 52,90
extra person	€ 5,60 - € 13,20
child (3-12 yrs)	€ 4,00 - € 9,90
dog (not July/Aug)	no charge

Special low season deals.

Italy – Muravera

Camping Capo Ferrato

Localitá Costa Rei, Via delle Ginestre, I-09040 Castiadas (Sardinia)
t: 070 991 012   e: info@campingcapoferrato.it
alanrogers.com/IT69770   www.campingcapoferrato.it

Accommodation: ☑ Pitch   ☑ Mobile home/chalet   ○ Hotel/B&B   ○ Apartment

Situated at the southern end of the magnificent Costa Rei, this small, friendly and well managed site has 83 touring pitches, many in great positions on the fine, white sand beachfront. They all have 3/6A electricity, are on sand, shady and of generous proportions. On the fringes of Costa Rei, the site benefits from close proximity to the shops and restaurants, yet enjoys absolute tranquillity. The charming restaurant holds it own against the village competition. This site is brilliant for beach lovers and windsurfers, and offers many watersports. It is reasonably priced and the beach shelves safely for children. The same family have been here since 1965 and the campsite was one of the first in Sardinia. In low season, special events are organised with other southern sites to enable you to 'feel the traditions' of Sardinia. Ask about the 'plein air' organisation. Close by is the Sette Fratelli Park with its mountains, canyons and woods, where you might be lucky enough to spot one of the many Sardinian deer.

You might like to know

The campsite overlooks the beautiful white sand and crystal clear waters of Costa Rei beach, which shelves gradually and is safe for children. Nearby 'Peppino's rock' marks a shallow bay ideal for snorkelling.

- ☑ Beach on site
- ☑ Beach within 1 km
- ☑ Sandy beach
- ○ Blue Flag quality
- ☑ Lifeguard *(high season)*
- ☑ Sun lounger and/or deckchair hire
- ○ Watersports *(e.g. sailing or windsurfing)*
- ☑ Snacks and drinks
- ☑ Sunshades/sunbeds
- ○ Dogs allowed *(on the beach)*

Facilities: Twenty toilet blocks all with WCs, showers and washbasins. New bathrooms. Bar. Restaurant and takeaway. Swimming and paddling pools (10/6-15/9). Tennis. Bicycle hire. Watersports incl. windsurfing school. Cinema. TV in bar. WiFi. Entertainment for children. Dogs are not accepted. A new play area for children has been added. Beach volleyball. WiFi. Off site: Fishing. Riding 500 m. Boat launching 4 km. Golf 40 km.

Open: 15 May - 30 September.

Directions: From Bari take the Brindisi road to Lecce, then SS101 to Gallipoli, then the SR274 towards Santa Maria di Leuca. Continue to Felline exit, and continue towards Torre San Giovanni, following the signs for Riva di Ugento. Site is well signed, turn right at traffic lights on SS19.

GPS: 39.87475, 18.141117

Charges guide

Per unit incl. 2 persons, 1 child
and electricity € 21,00 - € 45,00

extra person (over 2 yrs) € 5,00 - € 12,00

Italy – Ugento

Camping Riva di Ugento

Litoranea Gallipoli, Santa Maria di Leuca, I-73059 Ugento (Puglia)
t: 083 393 3600   e: info@rivadiugento.it
alanrogers.com/IT68650 www.rivadiugento.it

Accommodation: ☑ Pitch ☑ Mobile home/chalet ○ Hotel/B&B ○ Apartment

There are some campsites where you can be comfortable, have all the amenities at hand and still feel you are connecting with nature. Under the pine and eucalyptus trees of the Bay of Taranto foreshore is Camping Riva di Ugento. Its 850 pitches are nestled in and around the sand dunes and the foreshore area. They have space and trees around them and the sizes differ as the environment dictates the shape of most. The sea is only a short walk from most pitches and some are at the water's edge. The site buildings resemble huge wooden umbrellas and are in sympathy with the environment. There are swimming and paddling pools, although these are expensive to use in high season. A free cinema shows special events via satellite TV near the main bar and restaurant area. The area is sandy but well shaded, and the sea breezes scented with pine give the site a cool, fresh feel. This site has an isolated, natural ambiance that defies its size.

You might like to know

The white sandy beach stretches for miles along the idyllic Salento peninsula. It slopes gently into the crystal-clear sea making it ideal for families with children, and for couples to enjoy a romantic stroll at sunset.

- ☑ Beach on site
- ○ Beach within 1 km
- ☑ Sandy beach
- ○ Blue Flag quality
- ☑ Lifeguard *(high season)*
- ☑ Sun lounger and/or deckchair hire
- ○ Watersports *(e.g. sailing or windsurfing)*
- ☑ Snacks and drinks
- ☑ Sunshades/sunbeds
- ○ Dogs allowed *(on the beach)*

Facilities:

Facilities: The sixteen sanitary blocks are clean and good quality. Children's facilities and baby care areas, some Turkish style WCs, hot showers, with some blocks providing facilities for disabled visitors. Three supermarkets sell most everyday requirements. Fresh fish shop. Four restaurants, bars and snack bars and fast food outlets. Swimming pool and two paddling pools. Sandpit and play areas, with entertainment for all in high season. Tennis. Bicycle hire. Watersports. Boat hire. Minigolf. Riding. Internet café. Jetty and ramp for boats. WiFi (free). Mobile homes for rent (Istria Prestige). Dogs are accepted in certain areas. Off site: Hourly bus service from the reception area. Fishing. Riding 500 m. Golf 2 km. Nearest large supermarket in Novigrad 9 km.

Open: 1 April - 10 October.

Directions: The turn to Lanterna is well signed off the Novigrad to Porec road 8 km. south of Novigrad. Continue for 2 km. along the turn off road towards the coast and the campsite is on the right hand side.

GPS: 45.29672, 13.59442

Charges guide

Per unit incl. 2 persons and electricity	€ 16,90 - € 31,00
with full services	€ 18,30 - € 32,60
extra person	€ 4,40 - € 7,90
child (4-10 yrs)	no charge - € 5,40

Prices for pitches by the sea are higher.

Croatia – Porec

Camping Lanterna

Lanterna 1, Tar-Vabriga, HR-52465 Porec (Istria)
t: 052 465 010 e: camping@valamar.com
alanrogers.com/CR6716 www.camping-adriatic.com

Accommodation: ☑ Pitch ☑ Mobile home/chalet ○ Hotel/B&B ○ Apartment

This is a well organised site, one of the largest in Croatia with high standards and an amazing selection of activities, and is part of the Camping on the Adriatic group. Set in 80 hectares with over 3 km. of beach, there are 2,851 pitches, of which 1,887 are for touring units. All have electricity (10A) and fresh water, and 225 also have waste water drainage. Pitches are 80-120 sq.m. with some superb locations right on the sea, although these tend to be taken first so it is advisable to book ahead. Some of the better pitches are in a reserved booking area. There are wonderful coastal views from some of the well shaded terraced pitches. Facilities at Lanterna are impressive with the whole operation running smoothly for the campers. The land is sloping in parts and terraced in others. There is a pool complex, including a large pool for children, in addition to the bay with its rocky beaches and buoyed safety areas. Some of the marked and numbered pitches are shaded and arranged to take advantage of the topography. A member of Leading Campings group.

You might like to know

A vast array of sports and watersports is available, both at the campsite and at the nearby Valeta Sport Centre.

- ☑ Beach on site
- ○ Beach within 1 km
- ○ Sandy beach
- ☑ Blue Flag quality
- ○ Lifeguard *(high season)*
- ○ Sun lounger and/or deckchair hire
- ☑ Watersports *(e.g. sailing or windsurfing)*
- ○ Snacks and drinks
- ☑ Sunshades/sunbeds
- ☑ Dogs allowed *(on the beach)*

Facilities: Fifteen toilet blocks of varying styles and ages provide toilets, open style washbasins and controllable hot showers. Child size toilets, basins and showers. Bathroom (free). Facilities for disabled visitors. Laundry with sinks and washing machines. Two supermarkets. Souvenir shops and newspaper kiosk. Bars and restaurants with dance floor and stage. Patisserie. Tennis. Minigolf. Fishing (with permit). Bicycle hire. Games room. Marina with boat launching. Boat and pedalo hire. Disco outside entrance. Daily entertainment programme for children up to 12 yrs. Excursions organised. Off site: Riding 2 km.

Open: 25 April - 3 October.

Directions: Site is 2 km. north of Vrsar. Follow campsite signs from Vrsar.

GPS: 45.16522, 13.60723

Charges guide

Per unit incl. 2 persons and electricity	€ 17,70 - € 36,00
extra person	€ 6,50 - € 9,00
child (5-18 yrs)	no charge - € 7,20
dog	€ 2,50 - € 6,50

Croatia – Vrsar

Camping Valkanela

Valkanela, HR-52450 Vrsar (Istria)
t: 052 445 216 e: valkanela@maistra.hr
alanrogers.com/CR6727 www.campingrovinjvrsar.com

Accommodation: ☑ Pitch ○ Mobile home/chalet ○ Hotel/B&B ○ Apartment

Camping Valkanela is located in a beautiful green bay, right on the Adriatic Sea, between the villages of Vrsar and Funtana. It offers 1,300 pitches, all with 10A electricity. Pitches near the beach are numbered, have shade from mature trees and are slightly sloping towards the sea. Those towards the back of the site are on open fields without much shade and are not marked or numbered. Unfortunately, the number of pitches has increased dramatically over the years, many are occupied by seasonal campers and statics, and these parts of the site are not very attractive. Most numbered pitches have water points close by, but the back pitches have to go to the toilet blocks for water. For those who like activity, Valkanela has four gravel tennis courts, beach volleyball and opportunities for diving, water skiing and boat rental. There is a little marina for mooring small boats and a long rock and pebble private beach with some grass lawns for sunbathing. There may be some noise nuisance from the disco outside the entrance and during high season the site can become very crowded.

You might like to know

There are several beaches along the coastline between Vrsar and Funtana, including stone, pebble and sandy beaches.

- ☑ Beach on site
- ○ Beach within 1 km
- ○ Sandy beach
- ☑ Blue Flag quality
- ○ Lifeguard *(high season)*
- ☑ Sun lounger and/or deckchair hire
- ○ Watersports *(e.g. sailing or windsurfing)*
- ○ Snacks and drinks
- ○ Sunshades/sunbeds
- ☑ Dogs allowed *(on the beach)*

Facilities: Six modern and one refurbished toilet blocks with British style toilets, open washbasins and controllable hot showers. Child size facilities. Baby rooms. Family bathroom. Facilities for disabled visitors. Laundry service. Fridge box hire. Motorcaravan services. Shop. Two bar/restaurants. Large swimming pool. Playground. Fishing. Boat and pedalo hire. Miniclub (5-11 yrs). Excursions. Internet access in reception. WiFi. Off site: Riding 2 km. Rovinj 5 km.

Open: 21 April - 1 October.

Directions: Site is on the coast 4 km. southeast of Rovinj. From Rovinj travel south towards Pula. After 4 km. turn right following campsite signs.

GPS: 45.05432, 13.68568

Charges guide

Per person € 5,00 - € 10,00	
child (5-18 yrs) no charge - € 8,00	
pitch incl. electricity € 7,00 - € 20,00	
dog € 3,10 - € 6,50	

Croatia – Rovinj

Camping Vestar

Vestar bb, HR-52210 Rovinj (Istria)
t: 052 803 700 e: vestar@maistra.hr
alanrogers.com/CR6733 www.campingrovinjvrsar.com

Accommodation: ☑ Pitch ☑ Mobile home/chalet ○ Hotel/B&B ○ Apartment

Camping Vestar, just 5 km. from the historic harbour town of Rovinj, is one of the rare sites in Croatia with a partly sandy beach. Right behind the beach is a large area, attractively landscaped with young trees and shrubs, with grass for sunbathing. The site has 650 large pitches, of which 500 are for tourers, all with 6/10A electricity (the rest being taken by seasonal units and 60 pitches for tour operators). It is largely wooded with good shade and from the bottom row of pitches there are views of the sea. Pitching is on two separate fields, one for free camping, the other with numbered pitches. The pitches at the beach are in a half circle around the shallow bay, making it safe for children to swim. Vestar has a small marina and a jetty for mooring small boats and excursions to the islands are arranged. There is a miniclub and live music with dancing at one of the two bar/restaurants in the evenings. The restaurants all have open-air terraces, one covered with vines to protect you from the hot sun.

You might like to know

The beach (half pebble, half sand) is situated 5 km. from Rovinj.

☑ Beach on site
○ Beach within 1 km
☑ Sandy beach
☑ Blue Flag quality
○ Lifeguard *(high season)*
○ Sun lounger and/or deckchair hire
☑ Watersports *(e.g. sailing or windsurfing)*
○ Snacks and drinks
○ Sunshades/sunbeds
○ Dogs allowed *(on the beach)*

Croatia – Cres

Camping Kovacine

Melin I/20, HR-51557 Cres (Kvarner)
t: 051 573 150   e: campkovacine@kovacine.com
alanrogers.com/CR6765   www.camp-kovacine.com

Accommodation: ⊘ Pitch ⊘ Mobile home/chalet ○ Hotel/B&B ○ Apartment

Camping Kovacine is located on a peninsula on the beautiful Kvarner island of Cres, just 2 km. from the town of the same name. The site has 1002 numbered, mostly level pitches, of which 952 are for tourers (300 with 12A electricity). On sloping ground, partially shaded by mature olive and pine trees, pitching is on the large, open spaces between the trees. Some places have views of the Valun lagoon. Kovacine is partly an FKK (naturist) site, which is quite common in Croatia, and has a pleasant atmosphere. Here one can enjoy local live music on a stage close to the pebble beach (Blue Flag), where there is also a restaurant and bar. The site has its own beach, part concrete, part pebbles, and a jetty for mooring boats and fishing. It is close to the historic town of Cres, the main town on the island, which offers a rich history of fishing, shipyards and authentic Kvarner-style houses. There are also several bars, restaurants and shops.

You might like to know

For stays of ten consecutive days, the site refunds the cost of a one way ferry journey to the island of Cres; or the cost of a return journey for 18 consecutive days.

- ⊘ Beach on site
- ○ Beach within 1 km
- ○ Sandy beach
- ⊘ Blue Flag quality
- ⊘ Lifeguard *(high season)*
- ○ Sun lounger and/or deckchair hire
- ⊘ Watersports *(e.g. sailing or windsurfing)*
- ⊘ Snacks and drinks
- ○ Sunshades/sunbeds
- ⊘ Dogs allowed *(on the beach)*

Facilities: Modern, comfortable toilet blocks (two refurbished) offer British style toilets, equipped with solar power, open plan washbasins (some cabins for ladies) and hot showers. Private family bathroom for hire. Facilities for disabled visitors plus facilities for children. Laundry sinks and washing machine. Fridge box hire. Motorcaravan service point. Car wash. Mini-marina and boat crane. Supermarket, bar (Easter-19/10). Restaurant and pizzeria (May-15/10). Playground. Daily children's club. Evening shows with live music. Boat launching. Fishing. Diving centre. Motorboat hire. WiFi (free). Airport transfers. Off site: Wellness and fitness centre 0.5 km. Historic town of Cres with bars, restaurants and shops 2 km.

Open: 11 April - 19 October.

Directions: From Rijeka take no. 2 road south towards Labin and take ferry to Cres at Brestova. Continue to Cres and follow site signs.

GPS: 44.96188, 14.39650

Charges guide

Per unit incl. 2 persons and electricity	€ 17,80 - € 36,20
extra person	€ 6,00 - € 12,20
child (3-12 yrs)	€ 2,80 - € 5,00
dog	no charge - € 3,00

Camp Adriatic

Huljerat bb, HR-22202 Primosten (Dalmatia)
t: 022 571 223 e: info@camp-adriatic.hr
alanrogers.com/CR6845 www.camp-adriatic.hr

Accommodation: ⦿ Pitch ⦿ Mobile home/chalet ○ Hotel/B&B ○ Apartment

As we drove south down the Dalmatian coast road, we looked across a clear turquoise bay and saw a few tents, caravans and motorcaravans camped under some trees. A short distance later we were at the entrance of Camp Adriatic. With 530 pitches that slope down to the sea, the site is deceptive and enjoys a one kilometre beach frontage which is ideal for snorkelling and diving. Most pitches are level and have shade from pine trees. There are 212 numbered pitches and 288 unnumbered, all with 10/16A electricity. Close to the delightful town of Primosten (with a taxi boat service in high season) the site boasts good modern amenities and a fantastic location.

You might like to know

The site boasts its own diving centre, and can also organise boat trips and inland excursions to the beautiful Krka River national park and the Skardinski Buk waterfalls.

- ☑ Beach on site
- ○ Beach within 1 km
- ○ Sandy beach
- ○ Blue Flag quality
- ○ Lifeguard *(high season)*
- ☑ Sun lounger and/or deckchair hire
- ☑ Watersports *(e.g. sailing or windsurfing)*
- ○ Snacks and drinks
- ☑ Sunshades/sunbeds
- ○ Dogs allowed *(on the beach)*

Facilities: Four modern sanitary blocks provide clean toilets, hot showers and washbasins. Facilities for disabled visitors. Bathroom for children. Washing machine and dryer. Kitchen facilities. Small supermarket (15/5-30/9). Restaurant, bar and takeaway (all season). Sports centre. Miniclub. Beach. Diving school. Sailing school and boat hire. Entertainment programme in July/Aug. WiFi in reception area (charged). Off site: Primosten 2.5 km. Riding 15 km. Sibenic 25 km.

Open: 1 May - 15 October.

Directions: Take the A1 motorway south and leave at the Sibenik exit. Follow the 33 road into Sibenik and then go south along the coast road (no. 8), signed Primosten. Site is 2.5 km. north of Primosten.
GPS: 43.606517, 15.92095

Charges guide

Per person	Kn 34 - 60
child (3-12 yrs)	Kn 25 - 45
pitch incl. car and electricity	Kn 54 - 105
dog	Kn 18 - 32

Facilities:
Three excellent toilet blocks include showers, WCs and washbasins. Kitchen with sinks, electric hobs and fridges. Laundry with washing machines. Chemical disposal. Small shop and restaurant. Sandy beach. Fishing, sailing and swimming. Communal barbecues. Free WiFi over part of site. Bungalows to rent. Dogs are not allowed on the beach. Off site: Riding, golf and bicycle hire 10 km. Sithonia, Mount Athos and the nearby Spalathronisia islands.

Open: 1 May - 31 October.

Directions: Although the postal address is Neos Marmaras the site is 12 km. south. Stay on main coast road, past casino resort at Porto Carras and 5 km. further on turn right towards the site (signed). Then turn right again down to coast and turn left and on for 1.5 km. Turn right into site access road. Reception is 700 m.

GPS: 40.024183, 23.81595

Charges guide

Per unit incl. 2 persons
and electricity € 34,20 - € 38,00

No credit cards.

Greece – Neos Marmaras

Camping Areti

GR-63081 Neos Marmaras (Central Macedonia)
t: 237 507 1430   e: info@areti-chalkidiki.gr
alanrogers.com/GR8145   www.areti-campingandbungalows.gr

Accommodation: ☑ Pitch ☑ Mobile home/chalet ○ Hotel/B&B ○ Apartment

If you imagine a typical Greek campsite as being set immediately behind a small sandy beach in a quiet cove with pitches amongst pine and olive trees that stretch a long way back to the small coast road, then you have found your ideal site. Camping Areti is beautifully located just off the beaten track on the peninsula of Sithonia. It has 130 pitches for touring units. The olive groves at the rear provide hidden parking spaces for caravans and boats, and small boats can be launched from the beach. The Charalambidi family maintain their site to very high standards and visitors will not be disappointed. Olive, pine and eucalyptus trees provide shade for the grassed pitches, and when we visited in mid-June there was a wonderful display of cacti in full bloom by the entrance. The site, with its quiet, picturesque location, good facilities and friendly management has justly won many recommendations, and represents camping at its best; it is the ideal place to spend some time after the long journey down to Greece.

You might like to know

The Spalathronisia, three small islands ideal for excursions and fishing, are just 300 m. from the beach.

○ Beach on site
☑ Beach within 1 km
☑ Sandy beach
○ Blue Flag quality
○ Lifeguard *(high season)*
○ Sun lounger and/or deckchair hire
☑ Watersports *(e.g. sailing or windsurfing)*
☑ Snacks and drinks
○ Sunshades/sunbeds
○ Dogs allowed *(on the beach)*

Facilities: The good toilet block includes showers, WCs and washbasins. Facilities for disabled visitors. Kitchen includes sinks, electric hobs and fridges. Laundry. Chemical disposal. Bar, small shop and restaurant. Accommodation to rent. Off site: Finikounda and the Inouse Islands. Distance to boat launching and sailing 3 km. Bicycle hire 25 km.

Open: All year.

Directions: Site is 3 km. from the centre of Finikounda. From the village head west and turn left into the site.

GPS: 36.802817, 21.78105

Charges guide

Per unit incl. 2 persons
and electricity € 21,00 - € 24,00

extra person € 5,50 - € 6,00

child (4-10 yrs) € 3,00 - € 3,50

No credit cards.

Greece – Finikounda

Camping Finikes

GR-24006 Finikounda (Peloponnese)
t: 272 302 8524 e: camping-finikes@otenet.gr
alanrogers.com/GR8695 www.finikescamping.gr

Accommodation: ☑ Pitch ☑ Mobile home/chalet ○ Hotel/B&B ☑ Apartment

This site offers 80 level pitches with good shade and great views. It also has 16 apartments to rent. Some pitches have high reed screens that give good protection from the blazing Greek sun and the turquoise sea is great for swimming, windsurfing and sailing. The site is at the western corner of Finikounda Bay and has direct access to the sandy beach by crossing small natural dunes. The facilities are excellent and in low season, when there are 18 or less campers, each camper is given the keys to a WC and shower for their own personal use. The small picturesque village, three kilometres to the east, is at the back of the bay. Caiques and fishing boats are drawn up all along the sandy shore here, while tavernas serve their fresh catch along the water's edge.

You might like to know

An attractive path runs across the dunes from the site to the beach, which is excellent for children. The town of Finikounda is a 20-minute walk along the beach.

☑ Beach on site
○ Beach within 1 km
☑ Sandy beach
○ Blue Flag quality
○ Lifeguard *(high season)*
○ Sun lounger and/or deckchair hire
☑ Watersports *(e.g. sailing or windsurfing)*
○ Snacks and drinks
○ Sunshades/sunbeds
○ Dogs allowed *(on the beach)*

Facilities: Excellent refurbished toilet blocks include showers, WCs and washbasins. Baby bath. Facilities for disabled visitors. Chemical disposal. Laundry with washing machines and ironing board. Electric hobs for cooking. Fridge and freezer. Small shop (1/6-30/9).
Off site: Drepano beach, local tavernas and bars. Assini.

Open: 1 April - 30 October.

Directions: From Nafplio follow the main road west and then turn right towards Drepano. In the town follow the signs Plaka Drepano and turn left towards the coast. At the beach turn right and site is just ahead.

GPS: 37.53202, 22.89165

Charges guide

Per unit incl. 2 persons and electricity € 24,00

Greece – Nafplio

Camping Triton II

Plaka Drepano, GR-21060 Nafplio (Peloponnese)
t: 27 52 09 21 28
alanrogers.com/GR8635 www.tritonii.gr

Accommodation: ☑ Pitch ☑ Mobile home/chalet ○ Hotel/B&B ○ Apartment

What do we look for in a good campsite in Greece? Given the excellent Greek weather, the answer is probably a good, flat pitch with some shade, excellent toilets and showers that are spotlessly clean, a small shop and proximity to a beach and local tavernas. Well, here you have it all! Under the control of the owners, Mr. and Mrs. George Christopoulous, this is an exceptional site with 40 good sized touring pitches under high screens, just across the road from Drepano beach. Local tavernas are within strolling distance and the town's shops are about a mile away. Personal management and supervision clearly works and this small site sets very high standards that others often fail to achieve.

You might like to know

Close to the Drepano beach are small pool areas where blue and white cranes live and breed. Deprano village is 1.2 km. away with a choice of tavernas and local bars.

○ Beach on site
☑ Beach within 1 km
☑ Sandy beach
○ Blue Flag quality
○ Lifeguard *(high season)*
○ Sun lounger and/or deckchair hire
☑ Watersports *(e.g. sailing or windsurfing)*
○ Snacks and drinks
☑ Sunshades/sunbeds
○ Dogs allowed *(on the beach)*

Facilities: The five toilet blocks are well situated and, even in high season, were kept very clean and never became overcrowded. There are open washbasins, hot water to showers, and communal refrigerators and freezers. A small shop sells basic provisions. Other shops within walking distance. Dogs are accepted but must be kept on a lead and out of the sea.
Off site: Within walking distance of Gialova with its promenade restaurants. Pylos 6 km. Nestors Palace 12 km. Numerous places to visit.

Open: All year, full facilities April - October.

Directions: Directly on the National Road Pylos Kyparissia. 300 metres from the village of Gialova.

GPS: 36.94764, 21.70618

Charges guide

Per unit incl. 2 persons
and electricity € 22,00 - € 26,50

extra person € 5,50 - € 6,50

child € 2,50 - € 3,00

Greece – Pylos

Camping Navarino Beach

Gialova, GR-24001 Pylos (Peloponnese)
t: 272 302 2973 e: info@navarino-beach.gr
alanrogers.com/GR8705 www.navarino-beach.gr

Accommodation: ☑ Pitch ☑ Mobile home/chalet ◯ Hotel/B&B ◯ Apartment

There are 150 pitches, most facing the beach, with 30 being directly situated alongside. All have electricity (10A) and most have good shade. The pitches are arranged in rows to ensure that all have beach access. The facilities are adequate and cleaned regularly. The staff are friendly and efficient, and there is a very good restaurant with a terrace directly by the beach. The light wind in the morning, which strengthens on some afternoons, makes it a great windsurfing location and boats can be moored by the beach. This site is highly recommended. Situated directly on the beach in the historic Bay of Navarino, there can be very few sites in this guide that have the wonderful position this one occupies. It is superb and has the most amazing sunset to complement that. The site is split into two, with the section across the road used mainly for tents or as the overspill. There is plenty of shade. The beach is sandy and shelves gently making it incredibly safe for children.

You might like to know

The shallow blue water on this sandy beach is safe for children. The campsite recommend a visit to the Divary Lagoon, considered to be one of the most important lagoons in Greece.

☑ Beach on site
◯ Beach within 1 km
☑ Sandy beach
◯ Blue Flag quality
◯ Lifeguard *(high season)*
◯ Sun lounger and/or deckchair hire
☑ Watersports *(e.g. sailing or windsurfing)*
◯ Snacks and drinks
☑ Sunshades/sunbeds
☑ Dogs allowed *(on the beach)*

46

Balatontourist Camping Napfény

Halász ut. 5, H-8253 Révfülöp (Veszprem County)
t: 87 563 031   e: napfeny@balatontourist.hu
alanrogers.com/HU5370   www.balatontourist.hu

Accommodation: ☑ Pitch   ☑ Mobile home/chalet   ○ Hotel/B&B   ○ Apartment

Camping Napfény, an exceptionally good site, is designed for families with children of all ages looking for an active holiday, and has a 200 m. frontage on Lake Balaton. The site's 370 pitches vary in size (60-110 sq.m) and almost all have shade – very welcome during the hot Hungarian summers – and 6-10A electricity. As with most of the sites on Lake Balaton, a train line runs just outside the site boundary. There are steps to get into the lake and canoes, boats and pedaloes for hire. An extensive entertainment programme is designed for all ages and there are several bars and restaurants of various styles. There are souvenir shops and a supermarket. In fact, you need not leave the site at all during your holiday, although there are several excursions on offer, including to Budapest or to one of the many Hungarian spas, a trip over Lake Balaton or a traditional wine tour.

You might like to know

There are grassy beaches at the lakeside, where pedaloes and boats are for hire. Fishing is also popular on the lake.

- ☑ Beach on site
- ○ Beach within 1 km
- ○ Sandy beach
- ○ Blue Flag quality
- ○ Lifeguard *(high season)*
- ○ Sun lounger and/or deckchair hire
- ☑ Watersports *(e.g. sailing or windsurfing)*
- ○ Snacks and drinks
- ○ Sunshades/sunbeds
- ○ Dogs allowed *(on the beach)*

Facilities: The three excellent, well equipped sanitary blocks have child-size toilets and washbasins. Two bathrooms (hourly charge). Heated baby room. Facilities for disabled campers. Launderette. Dog shower. Motorcaravan services. Supermarket, souvenir shop and several bars (all 1/6-31/8). Restaurants. Children's pool (1/6-31/8). Massage. Hairdresser. Sports field. Minigolf. Fishing. Bicycle hire. Canoe, rowing boat and pedalo hire. Extensive entertainment programme for all ages. WiFi throughout (one free zone, elsewhere charged). Off site: Riding 3 km. Golf 20 km.

Open: 25 April - 28 September.

Directions: Follow road 71 from Veszprém southeast to Keszthely. Site is in Révfülöp.
GPS: 46.829469, 17.640164

Charges guide

Per unit incl. 2 persons and electricity	HUF 3750 - 7300
extra person	HUF 900 - 1250
child (2-14 yrs)	HUF 550 - 1000
dog	HUF 550 - 1000

Facilities: The six toilet blocks (three heated) are of exemplary quality. Washing machines and dryers. Motorcaravan services. Gas supplies. Supermarket, restaurant, bar and takeaway (all season). Snack kiosk at beach. Lifeguards on duty. Tennis. Minigolf. Bicycle hire. Canoe and pedalo hire. Boat launching. Playgrounds. Doctor calls. Dogs are not accepted. New chalet for disabled visitors. Camping accessories shop. Car hire. Car wash. WiFi (charged). Off site: Fishing 500 m. Water-skiing and windsurfing 1 km. Riding 5 km. Golf 8 km. Boatyard with maintenance facilities.

Open: 27 March - 31 October.

Directions: On the Bellinzona-Locarno road 13, exit Tenero. Site is signed at roundabout. Coming from the south, enter Tenero and follow signs to site.

GPS: 46.168611, 8.855556

Charges guide

Per unit incl. 2 persons
and electricity CHF 39,00 - 90,00

extra person CHF 9,00 - 11,00

Some pitches have min. stay regulations. Discounts for stays over 10 days.

Switzerland – Tenero

Camping Campofelice

Via alle Brere 7, CH-6598 Tenero (Ticino)
t: 091 745 1417 e: camping@campofelice.ch
alanrogers.com/CH9890 www.campofelice.ch

Accommodation: ☑ Pitch ◯ Mobile home/chalet ◯ Hotel/B&B ◯ Apartment

The largest site in Switzerland, it is bordered on the front by Lake Maggiore and on one side by the Verzasca estuary, where the site has its own marina. Campofelice is divided into rows, with 860 generously sized, individual pitches on flat grass on either side of hard access roads. Mostly well shaded, all pitches have electricity connections (10-13A) and 409 also have water, drainage and TV connections. Pitches near the lake cost more (these are not available for motorcaravans until September) and a special area is reserved for small tents. The sheer quality of this superb site justifies the higher than average prices. Sporting facilities are good and there are cycle paths in the area, including into Locarno. The beach by the lake is sandy, long and wider than the usual lakeside ones. It shelves gently so that bathing is safe for children. Within a demarcated area are floating trampolines and rafts, and a specially marked section for toddlers.

You might like to know

The site lies on the sandy shores of Lake Maggiore, where there is safe swimming and a private beach. Kayaks and canoes are available to hire from the site's own harbour.

- ☑ Beach on site
- ◯ Beach within 1 km
- ☑ Sandy beach
- ◯ Blue Flag quality
- ☑ Lifeguard *(high season)*
- ◯ Sun lounger and/or deckchair hire
- ☑ Watersports *(e.g. sailing or windsurfing)*
- ☑ Snacks and drinks
- ◯ Sunshades/sunbeds
- ◯ Dogs allowed *(on the beach)*

Facilities: Each area has one large and one small sanitary block. Heated block near reception. Cleaned twice daily, they include facilities for disabled visitors and babies. Launderette. Supermarket, bakery, beach shop (all 15/4-15/9). Restaurant, bar and takeaway (all 15/4-15/9). Swimming pool (heated 15/6-15/9). Steam room. Tennis. Bicycle hire. Play area. TV room and library. Internet terminal. WiFi throughout (charged). Charcoal and electric barbecues are not permitted. Dogs are not accepted 26/6-5/9. Off site: Fishing 200 m. Riding 500 m. Golf 20 km.

Open: 2 April - 9 October.

Directions: From Royan centre take coast road (D25) along the seafront of St Georges-de-Didonne towards Meschers. Site is signed at roundabout at end of the main beach.

GPS: 45.583583, -0.986533

Charges guide

Per unit incl. 3 persons and electricity	€ 15,00 - € 46,00
extra person	€ 6,00 - € 11,00
child (under 7 yrs)	no charge - € 7,00
dog (not 6/7-1/9)	€ 6,00 - € 7,00

Less 20% outside July/Aug.

France – Saint Georges-de-Didonne

Camping Bois Soleil

2 avenue de Suzac, F-17110 Saint Georges-de-Didonne (Charente-Maritime)
t: 05 46 05 05 94   e: camping.bois.soleil@wanadoo.fr
alanrogers.com/FR17010 www.bois-soleil.com

Accommodation: ☑ Pitch ☑ Mobile home/chalet ○ Hotel/B&B ○ Apartment

Close to the sea, Bois Soleil is a large site in three parts, with 165 serviced pitches for touring units and a few for tents. All the touring pitches are hedged and have electricity (6/10A), with water and drainage between two. The main part, Les Pins, is attractive with trees and shrubs providing shade. Opposite is La Mer with direct access to the beach, some areas with less shade and an area for tents. The third part, La Forêt, is for caravan holiday homes. It is best to book your preferred area as it can be full mid June to late August. Excellent private sanitary facilities are available to rent, either on your pitch or at a block (subject to availability). There are a few pitches with lockable gates. The areas are all well tended and are cleared and raked between visitors. This lively site offers something for everyone, whether it be a beach-side spot or a traditional pitch, plenty of activities or the quiet life. Recent additions include a new toilet block and some accommodation to rent with sea views. The wide sandy beach is popular with children and provides a pleasant walk to the pretty town of Saint Georges-de-Didonne.

You might like to know

There are plenty of opportunities for sampling the regional specialities – seafood, oysters from Marennes-Oléron, Cognac and the well known Pineau des Charentes.

☑ Beach on site
○ Beach within 1 km
☑ Sandy beach
☑ Blue Flag quality
☑ Lifeguard *(high season)*
○ Sun lounger and/or deckchair hire
☑ Watersports *(e.g. sailing or windsurfing)*
☑ Snacks and drinks
☑ Sunshades/sunbeds
○ Dogs allowed *(on the beach)*

Facilities: Traditional style toilet facilities are kept to a high standard. Laundry facilities. Motorcaravan services. Well stocked shop with bakery and restaurant (1/4-15/9). Indoor pool with first class spa and wellness centre (all year, with professional staff). Outdoor pool (heated, 1/4-15/9). Bicycle hire. Children's clubs (July-Aug). Internet access and WiFi (charged). ATM. No charcoal barbecues. Off site: Beach 200 m and 400 m. via a sandy path. Bus service from Chéray. Fishing 2 km. Riding 2 km. Golf 12 km.

Open: April - October.

Directions: Cross the viaduct onto the Ile d'Oléron. Take D734 (St Georges-d'Oléron). At traffic lights in Chéray turn left. Follow signs for camping and Sable Vignier. Soon signs indicate directions to les Gros Joncs.

GPS: 45.95356, -1.37979

Charges guide

Per unit incl. 2 persons
and electricity € 19,60 - € 48,70

France – Saint Georges-d'Oléron

Camping les Gros Joncs

Les Sables Vignier B.P. 17, F-17190 Saint Georges-d'Oléron (Charente-Maritime)
t: 05 46 76 52 29   e: info@les-gros-joncs.fr
alanrogers.com/FR17070   www.camping-les-gros-joncs.com

Accommodation: ☑ Pitch   ☑ Mobile home/chalet   ○ Hotel/B&B   ○ Apartment

Situated on the west coast of the island of Ile d'Oléron, les Gros Joncs is owned and run by the Cavel family who work hard to keep the site up to date and of high quality. There are 50 or so touring pitches of a good size (some extra large) with tall pine trees providing a choice between full sun and varying degrees of shade. All have water and 10A electricity to hand. The main building not only houses a light and airy reception, but also a modern, beautifully presented bar and restaurant, a fully stocked and competitively priced shop, an attractive indoor swimming pool and a magnificent spa. The indoor pool, with water jets and jacuzzi, has glass sides which in good weather are opened out onto an outdoor pool area where there are also water slides, a paddling area and plenty of sunbathing terraces. Both pools are heated. The spa offers hydrotherapy and beauty treatments, sauna, and a comprehensive fitness room. Much attention has been given to the needs of disabled visitors here, including chalets where space and equipment are specially adapted. All the amenities are of a standard unusual on a campsite.

You might like to know

Our heated open-air pools include a toboggan, a large swimming pool and an adventure paddling pool. The indoor pool also has a whirlpool, lazy river, anatomical seats and powerful water jets.

☑ Beach on site
○ Beach within 1 km
☑ Sandy beach
○ Blue Flag quality
☑ Lifeguard *(high season)*
○ Sun lounger and/or deckchair hire
○ Watersports *(e.g. sailing or windsurfing)*
○ Snacks and drinks
○ Sunshades/sunbeds
☑ Dogs allowed *(on the beach)*

Camping l'Océan

50 route d'Ars, F-17670 La Couarde-sur-Mer (Charente-Maritime)
t: 05 46 29 87 70 e: info@campingocean.com
alanrogers.com/FR17230 www.campingocean.com

Accommodation: ☑ Pitch ☑ Mobile home/chalet ○ Hotel/B&B ○ Apartment

L'Océan lies close to the centre of the Ile de Ré, just 50 m. from a sandy beach. There are 338 pitches here with 161 for touring units, the remainder occupied by mobile homes and chalets. The camping area is well shaded and pitches are of a reasonable size, all with electricity (10A). A pleasant bar/restaurant overlooks the large heated swimming pool which is surrounded by an attractive sunbathing terrace. Bicycle hire is popular here as the island offers over 100 km. of interesting cycle routes. A bus goes to La Rochelle from 300 metres outside the site. In peak season a range of entertainment is organised including disco evenings.

You might like to know

A fine sandy beach is just 50 m. away. With over 100 km. of cycle paths, why not discover the magic of the Ile de Ré by bicycle?

○ Beach on site
☑ Beach within 1 km
☑ Sandy beach
○ Blue Flag quality
○ Lifeguard *(high season)*
○ Sun lounger and/or deckchair hire
☑ Watersports *(e.g. sailing or windsurfing)*
○ Snacks and drinks
○ Sunshades/sunbeds
○ Dogs allowed *(on the beach)*

Facilities: The two toilet blocks are modern and well maintained with facilities for children and disabled visitors. Laundry. Dog shower. Motorcaravan services. Shop. Bar, restaurant and takeaway. Swimming pool (27/4-29/9). Games room. Riding. Tennis. Fishing pond adjacent. Play area. Minigolf (free). Trampolines and bouncy castle. Boules. Multisports area. Entertainment in high season. Bicycle hire. No charcoal barbecues. Internet and WiFi (free). Mobile homes for rent. Off site: Jet ski hire adjacent. Beach 50 m. La Couarde 2.5 km. Golf 5 km.

Open: 27 April - 28 September.

Directions: After toll bridge, join D735 which runs along the north side of island until you pass La Couarde. The site is 2.5 km. beyond village (in direction of Ars-en-Ré).
GPS: 46.20433, -1.46767

Charges guide

Per unit incl. 1 or 2 persons and electricity € 25,00 - € 49,00	
extra person € 5,00 - € 11,00	
dog € 3,00 - € 5,00	

Facilities: Laundry facilities. Shop, restaurant, takeaway and bar with TV, heated outdoor swimming pool (all season). Play area. Children's club and entertainment (high season). Bicycle hire. Max. 1 dog. WiFi throughout. Only gas barbecues allowed. Communal barbecue provided. Off site: Riding 500 m. Beach, fishing, boat launching and sailing 800 m. Golf 20 km.

Open: 12 April - 21 September.

Directions: Over the toll bridge and turn left at second roundabout. Site is well signed.

GPS: 46.18461, -1.3080

Charges guide

Contact the site for details.

France – La Flotte-en-Ré

Camping les Peupliers

route de Rivedoux, F-17630 La Flotte-en-Ré (Charente-Maritime)
t: 02 51 20 41 94 e: contact@camp-atlantique.com
alanrogers.com/FR17290 www.camp-atlantique.com

Accommodation: ◯ Pitch ☑ Mobile home/chalet ◯ Hotel/B&B ◯ Apartment

On the Ile de Ré, les Peupliers is just 800 metres from the sea with sea views from some of the pitches. There are no touring pitches here, but it does offer 144 chalets for rent, in an area of light woodland with the trees providing some shade. English is spoken at reception and the staff go out of their way to make your stay enjoyable. The site is within walking distance of the shops and restaurants of the pretty fishing port of Flotte-en-Ré. With 100 km. of cycle tracks, sandy beaches, local markets and a uniquely sunny micro-climate, this is a great place to sample island life. Historic La Rochelle on the mainland is one of France's most captivating ports.

You might like to know

A fine sandy beach protected by dunes and pine trees is 800 m. from the site. Nearby, in Flotte-en-Ré, there is a sailing school, catamaran sailing trips and sea fishing.

◯ Beach on site
☑ Beach within 1 km
☑ Sandy beach
◯ Blue Flag quality
☑ Lifeguard *(high season)*
◯ Sun lounger and/or deckchair hire
☑ Watersports *(e.g. sailing or windsurfing)*
☑ Snacks and drinks
☑ Sunshades/sunbeds
☑ Dogs allowed *(on the beach)*

Facilities: The modern sanitary block is of a good standard and is kept clean and fresh. Cubicle with controllable shower and washbasin. Facilities for babies and disabled visitors. No chemical disposal point (drains on pitches used). Laundry. Bar and snack bar with takeaway. Two heated swimming pools (one will be covered for 2014). Paddling pool. Jacuzzi. Play area. Children's club and evening entertainment and activities for all the family (July/Aug). WiFi over site (charged July/Aug). Bicycle hire. Off site: Beach and fishing 150 m. Village with market (daily 15/6-15/9) 1 km. Riding 1.5 km. Sailing and boat launching 2.5 km. Golf 7 km.

Open: 6 April - 28 September.

Directions: Cross the bridge to the Ile d'Oléron and continue on the D26/D734 through St Pierre and St Georges, then turn right onto the D273E1 towards La Brée-les-Baines. Bear left at roundabout, then at T-junction turn left from where the campsite is signed.

GPS: 46.02007, -1.35764

Charges guide

Per unit incl. 2 persons and electricity	€ 23,10 - € 39,05
extra person	€ 7,75 - € 9,10
child (1-14 yrs)	€ 4,40 - € 5,70
dog	€ 4,30

France – La Brée-les-Bains

Antioche d'Oléron

16 route de Proires, F-17840 La Brée-les-Bains (Charente-Maritime)
t: 05 46 47 92 00   e: info@camping-antiochedoleron.com
alanrogers.com/FR17570   www.camping-antiochedoleron.com

Accommodation: ☑ Pitch ☑ Mobile home/chalet ○ Hotel/B&B ○ Apartment

Close to the northern point of the Ile d'Oléron, Antioche is quietly located within a five minute walk of the beach. There are 130 pitches, of which 87 are occupied by mobile homes, half available for rent, and 43 are for touring units. The pitches are set amongst attractive shrubs and palm trees and all have electricity (16A), water and a drain. The site becomes livelier in season with regular evening entertainment and activities for all the family. A thriving market selling local produce and products is within easy reach on foot, and is held daily in high season. Along the road at Saint Denis-d'Oléron is a busy port and marina with a choice of bars and restaurants, many specialising in seafood including local oysters and mussels. A short drive south takes you to Saint Georges, though for a better choice of shops and restaurants - and a hypermarket - head on to Saint Pierre. There is a good choice of sandy beaches, whilst across the salt marshes at Boyardville you can take out a canoe or go on a boat trip across to historical Fort Boyard, or to the Ile d'Aix.

You might like to know

One area of the beach is dedicated to watersports and pleasure boats. At low tide there is a flat, rocky area, perfect for fishing.

○ Beach on site
☑ Beach within 1 km
☑ Sandy beach
○ Blue Flag quality
☑ Lifeguard *(high season)*
○ Sun lounger and/or deckchair hire
☑ Watersports *(e.g. sailing or windsurfing)*
☑ Snacks and drinks
○ Sunshades/sunbeds
○ Dogs allowed *(on the beach)*

Camping Signol

121 avenue des Albatros, F-17190 Boyardville (Charente-Maritime)
t: 02 51 20 41 94 e: contact@camp-atlantique.com
alanrogers.com/FR17600 www.camp-atlantique.com

Accommodation: ☑ Pitch ☑ Mobile home/chalet ○ Hotel/B&B ○ Apartment

Occupying an eight-hectare site just 800 metres from the sandy beaches, and a short walk from the little port of Boyardville, this campsite has plenty to offer. Of the 340 pitches, just 52 are for touring, set amongst high pine trees, some occupying hillocks, others tucked away among mobile homes. The pitches vary in size and access to some is tight making them unsuitable for larger units. Levelling blocks may be required. Electricity (6A) is available to all, although long leads are sometimes required. There may be a short walk to the water supply. Boyardville lies on the east coast of the island and is approached across extensive salt marshes. From the shore, you look out across the bay towards Fouras and the estuary of the River Charente. Boat trips can be taken to Fort Boyard, and to the Ile d'Aix; in contrast, the salt marshes can be explored by canoe. Along the quayside is a range of boutiques, bars and restaurants, while a short drive away is the town of Saint Pierre-d'Oléron with a wider range of shops and eating places, plus a large hypermarket.

You might like to know

The beautiful fine-sand beaches of Boyardville are only 800 m. away, from where there is a wonderful view of Fort Boyard. Cycle tracks criss-cross the oyster canals and Saumonards Forest.

○ Beach on site
☑ Beach within 1 km
☑ Sandy beach
○ Blue Flag quality
☑ Lifeguard *(high season)*
○ Sun lounger and/or deckchair hire
☑ Watersports *(e.g. sailing or windsurfing)*
☑ Snacks and drinks
☑ Sunshades/sunbeds
☑ Dogs allowed *(on the beach)*

Facilities: Three traditional, fully equipped toilet blocks provide washbasins in cubicles and preset showers. There are basic facilities for campers with disabilities, and for children. Laundry. Motorcaravan services. Shop, bar/snack bar, takeaway (all season). Two heated swimming pools (indoor all season with sauna, steam room and fitness room; outdoor from 3/5). Massage and beauty parlour. Enclosed play area with seats for parents. Children's club (4-12 yrs, July/Aug). Boules. Evening entertainment (all season). WiFi throughout. Dogs are accepted (max. 1 per pitch). Only gas barbecues allowed (except on communal area). Mobile homes and chalets available to hire. Max. one dog. Off site: Fishing 500 m. Beach, sailing and windsurfing 800 m. Golf 2 km. Riding 4 km. Cycle and walking trails. St Pierre-d'Oléron (good choice of shops and restaurants and hypermarket) 8 km.

Open: 12 April - 21 September.

Directions: Cross the bridge to the Ile d'Oléron and continue on the D26/D734 to Dolus and turn right on D126 signed Boyardville. Continue on this road for 7 km. until the canal bridge at the edge of the town. Cross bridge and turn immediately sharp right along the quayside. Site signed from here.

GPS: 45.96807, -1.24456

Charges guide

Per unit incl. 2 persons and electricity	€ 22,00 - € 39,00
extra person	€ 5,00 - € 9,00
child (under 5 yrs)	no charge - € 6,00
dog	€ 5,00

Camping du Letty

Chemin de Creisanguer, F-29950 Bénodet (Finistère)
t: 02 98 57 04 69 e: reception@campingduletty.com
alanrogers.com/FR29030 www.campingduletty-benodet.com

Accommodation: ☑ Pitch ◯ Mobile home/chalet ◯ Hotel/B&B ◯ Apartment

Facilities: Six well placed toilet blocks are of good quality and include washbasins in large cabins and controllable hot showers (charged). One block includes a separate laundry and dog washing enclosures. Baby rooms. Separate facility for disabled visitors. Launderette. Hairdressing room. Motorcaravan service points. Well stocked shop. Extensive snack bar and takeaway. Bar with games room and night club. Library/reading room with four computer stations. Entertainment room with satellite TV. Pool complex with indoor and outdoor pools, children's pool, jacuzzi and slide. Fitness centre (no charge). Sauna and solarium (both charged). Tennis and squash (charged). Boules. Archery. Well equipped play area. Entertainment and activities (July/Aug). WiFi in reception (charged). Off site: Sailing, fishing, riding and golf all nearby. Bénodet and Quimper.

Open: 12 June - 6 September.

Directions: From N165 take D70 Concarneau exit. At first roundabout take D44 to Fouesnant. Turn right at T-junction. After 2 km. turn left to Fouesnant (still D44). Continue through La Forêt Fouesnant and Fouesnant, picking up signs for Bénodet. Shortly before Bénodet at roundabout turn left (Le Letty). Turn right at next mini-roundabout and site is 500 m. on left.

GPS: 47.86700, -4.08783

Charges guide

Per unit incl. 2 persons and electricity	€ 22,00 - € 39,50
extra person	€ 4,00 - € 9,00
child (2-6 yrs)	€ 2,00 - € 4,50
dog	€ 2,00 - € 3,00

The Guyader family have ensured that this excellent and attractive site has plenty to offer for all the family. With a charming ambience, the site on the outskirts of the popular resort of Bénodet spreads over 22 acres with 542 pitches, all for touring units. Groups of four to eight pitches are set in cul-de-sacs with mature hedging and trees to divide each group. All pitches have electricity (10A), water and drainage. As well as direct access to a small sandy beach, with a floating pontoon (safe bathing depends on the tides), the site has a grand aquatic parc, with heated open-air and indoor pools including children's pools, jacuzzi, and slides. At the attractive floral entrance, former farm buildings provide a host of facilities including an extensively equipped fitness room and new wellness rooms for massage and jacuzzis. There is also a modern, purpose built nightclub and bar providing high quality live entertainment most evenings (situated well away from most pitches to avoid disturbance).

You might like to know

Letty is beside La Mer Blanche, which empties and fills with the rhythm of the tides and is a haven for birds. The area is a paradise for walkers and nature lovers and has some wonderful sandy beaches.

- ☑ Beach on site
- ◯ Beach within 1 km
- ☑ Sandy beach
- ◯ Blue Flag quality
- ◯ Lifeguard *(high season)*
- ◯ Sun lounger and/or deckchair hire
- ☑ Watersports *(e.g. sailing or windsurfing)*
- ☑ Snacks and drinks
- ◯ Sunshades/sunbeds
- ☑ Dogs allowed *(on the beach)*

Facilities: Two clean, well maintained sanitary blocks include mixed style toilets, washbasins in cabins, baby baths and facilities for disabled visitors. Laundry room. Motorcaravan service point. Small shop (from 15/5). Bar and restaurant (from 1/6) with outside terrace and takeaway. Reading and TV room. Heated indoor and outdoor pools with sun terrace and paddling pool. Sauna (charged). Play areas. Games room. Various activities are organised in July/Aug. Internet access. WiFi (charged). Off site: Beach, fishing and watersports 300 m. Supermarket 3 km. Riding 4 km.

Open: 1 April - 30 September.

Directions: From N165 take D24 Kerampaou exit. After 3 km. turn right towards Nizon and bear right at church in village following signs to Névez (D77). Continue through Névez, following signs to Raguénès. Continue for 3 km. to site entrance on left (entrance is quite small and easy to miss).

GPS: 47.79337, -3.80049

Charges guide

Per unit incl. 2 persons and electricity	€ 20,30 - € 39,70
extra person	€ 4,40 - € 6,00
child (under 7 yrs)	no charge - € 3,90
dog	€ 1,50 - € 3,20

France – Névez

Camping le Raguénès-Plage

19 rue des Iles, F-29920 Névez (Finistère)
t: 02 98 06 80 69 e: info@camping-le-raguenes-plage.com
alanrogers.com/FR29090 www.camping-le-raguenes-plage.com

Accommodation: ☑ Pitch ☑ Mobile home/chalet ○ Hotel/B&B ○ Apartment

Mme. Guyader and her family will ensure you receive a warm welcome on arrival at this well kept and pleasant site. Le Raguénès-Plage is an attractive and well laid out campsite with many shrubs and trees. The 287 pitches are a good size, flat and grassy, separated by trees and hedges. All have electricity, water and drainage. The site is used by two tour operators (51 pitches), and has 61 mobile homes of its own. A pool complex complete with heated indoor pool and water toboggan is a key feature and is close to the friendly bar, restaurant, shop and takeaway. From the far end of the campsite a delightful five minute walk along a path and through a cornfield takes you down to a pleasant, sandy beach looking out towards the Ile Verte and the Presqu'île de Raguénès.

You might like to know

There is a heated, covered pool, and a separate outdoor pool, also heated, with water slide and paddling pool.

☑ Beach on site
○ Beach within 1 km
☑ Sandy beach
☑ Blue Flag quality
○ Lifeguard *(high season)*
○ Sun lounger and/or deckchair hire
☑ Watersports *(e.g. sailing or windsurfing)*
☑ Snacks and drinks
○ Sunshades/sunbeds
○ Dogs allowed *(on the beach)*

France – Landéda

Camping des Abers

Dunes de Sainte Marguerite, F-29870 Landéda (Finistère)
t: 02 98 04 93 35   e: camping-des-abers@wanadoo.fr
alanrogers.com/FR29130   www.camping-des-abers.com

Accommodation: ☑ Pitch ☑ Mobile home/chalet ○ Hotel/B&B ○ Apartment

This delightful 12-acre site is in a beautiful location almost at the tip of the Presqu'île Sainte Marguerite on the northwestern shores of Brittany. The peninsula lies between the mouths (abers) of two rivers, Aber Wrac'h and Aber Benoît. Camping des Abers is set just back from a wonderful sandy beach with rocky outcrops and islands you can walk to at low tide. There are 180 pitches (158 for touring), landscaped and terraced, some with amazing views, others sheltered by mature hedges, trees and flowering shrubs. Hubert le Cuff and his team make you very welcome and speak excellent English. This extensive site was created out of nothing by the le Cuff family who have tended it with loving care over the years. It is arranged on different levels avoiding any regimentation or crowding. Easily accessed by good internal roads, electricity is available to all (long leads may be needed). With its soft, white sandy beach the setting is ideal for those with younger children and this quiet, rural area provides a wonderful, tranquil escape from the hustle and bustle of life.

You might like to know

There is a sailing club five minutes drive from the site, and on the nearby estuary there are oyster farms and a bird sanctuary.

- ☑ Beach on site
- ○ Beach within 1 km
- ☑ Sandy beach
- ○ Blue Flag quality
- ○ Lifeguard *(high season)*
- ○ Sun lounger and/or deckchair hire
- ☑ Watersports *(e.g. sailing or windsurfing)*
- ○ Snacks and drinks
- ○ Sunshades/sunbeds
- ○ Dogs allowed *(on the beach)*

Facilities: Three toilet blocks provide washbasins in cubicles and showers (token from reception € 0.65-0.85). Facilities for disabled visitors and babies. Fully equipped laundry. Motorcaravan service point. Shop stocks essentials (14/5-22/9). Takeaway (1/7-31/8). Play area. Games room. Hairdresser. The site is famous for its Breton music and dancing, cooking classes and guided walks arranged. Splendid beach with good bathing, fishing, windsurfing and other watersports. WiFi throughout. Off site: Bus service just outside site. Pizzeria next door. Tennis nearby. Sailing club 3 km. Riding 7 km. Golf 30 km. Miles of superb coastal walks. The nearby town of L'Aber Wrac'h, a well known yachting centre, has many memorable restaurants.

Open: 1 May - 30 September.

Directions: Landéda is 55 km. west of Roscoff via D10 to Plougerneau then D13 crossing river bridge (Aber Wrac'h) and turning west to Lannilis. From N12 Morlaix-Brest road turn north on D59 to Lannilis. Continue through town taking road to Landéda and from there follow signs for Dunes de Ste Marguerite, Camping and des Abers.

GPS: 48.59344, -4.60281

Charges guide

Per unit incl. 2 persons and electricity	€ 15,30 - € 18,00
extra person	€ 3,40 - € 4,00
child (under 7 yrs)	€ 2,10 - € 2,50
dog	€ 1,90 - € 2,20

Facilities: Two modern sanitary blocks, recently completely renewed and heated in winter, include mainly British style toilets, some washbasins in cubicles, baby baths and good facilities for disabled visitors. Family bathrooms. Laundry facilities. Motorcaravan service point. Shop. Restaurant by entrance, bar and terrace, takeaway (13/4-15/9). Covered, heated swimming and paddling pools. Large games hall. Play area. Football field. Minigolf. Communal barbecue area. Daily activities for children and adults organised in July/Aug. Bicycle hire. Internet access and WiFi in reception area (charged). Off site: Nearby sea and river fishing and watersports. Beach 250 m. Riding 2 km. Golf 15 km.

Open: 12 April - 21 September.

Directions: From N165 take either exit for Kervidanou, Quimperlé Ouest or Kergostiou, Quimperlé Centre, Clohars Carnoët exit and follow D16 to Clohars Carnoët. Then take D24 for Le Pouldu and follow site signs in village.

GPS: 47.76867, -3.54508

Charges guide

Per unit incl. 2 persons and electricity	€ 16,50 - € 39,50
extra person	€ 4,00 - € 6,50
child (under 7 yrs)	€ 2,85 - € 4,00
dog	€ 2,80

France – Le Pouldu

Camping les Embruns

2 rue du Philosophe Alain, le Pouldu Plages, F-29360 Clohars-Carnoët (Finistère)
t: 02 98 39 91 07   e: camping-les-embruns@orange.fr
alanrogers.com/FR29180 www.camping-les-embruns.com

Accommodation: ☑ Pitch ☑ Mobile home/chalet ○ Hotel/B&B ○ Apartment

This site is unusual in that it is located in the heart of a village, yet is only 250 metres from a sandy cove. The entrance with its code operated barrier and wonderful floral displays, is the first indication that this is a well tended and well organised site, and the owners have won numerous regional and national awards for its superb presentation. The 176 pitches (100 occupied by mobile homes) are separated by trees, shrubs and bushes, and most have electricity (16A Europlug), water and drainage. There is a covered, heated swimming pool, a circular paddling pool and a water play pool and slide. A recent addition is the wellness centre with sauna and massage facilities. It is only a short walk to the village centre with all its attractions and services. It is also close to beautiful countryside and the Carnoët Forest which are good for walking and cycling.

You might like to know

Le Pouldu has three superb, sandy, south-facing beaches with good water quality, one just 250 m. from the campsite. There are many creeks, moorings, watersports opportunities, and sea and lake fishing.

- ○ Beach on site
- ☑ Beach within 1 km
- ☑ Sandy beach
- ☑ Blue Flag quality
- ☑ Lifeguard *(high season)*
- ○ Sun lounger and/or deckchair hire
- ☑ Watersports *(e.g. sailing or windsurfing)*
- ☑ Snacks and drinks
- ○ Sunshades/sunbeds
- ○ Dogs allowed *(on the beach)*

France – La Forêt-Fouesnant

Camping de Kéranterec

Route de Port la Forêt, F-29940 La Forêt-Fouesnant (Finistère)
t: 02 98 56 98 11   e: info@camping-keranterec.com
alanrogers.com/FR29240   www.camping-keranterec.com

Accommodation: ☑ Pitch   ☑ Mobile home/chalet   ◯ Hotel/B&B   ◯ Apartment

A well established family run site with a very French ambience, Kéranterec has 265 grassy pitches in two distinct areas. The upper part of the site is more open and has little shade, and is also largely taken up by private mobile homes. The lower and more mature area is predominantly for tourers, with terraced pitches set in a former orchard. Spacious and divided by mature hedging, all pitches have electrical connections (25 m. cable advised) and most also offer water and drainage. Some pitches have shade from the many trees on the lower part of the site, and some also overlook the little cove at the rear of the site. The trees still provide fruit for the cider produced on site (which we can highly recommend!). At the rear of the site a gate leads to a small beach and the coastal footpath to Concarneau (8 km). The area around La Forêt-Fouesnant is very much 'picture postcard' Brittany – plenty of enticing crêperies and seafood restaurants, enchanting mediaeval villages and towns and delightful hidden coves. For these and many other reasons, there are plenty of campsites to choose from and Camping de Kéranterec is well worth considering.

You might like to know

Walkers can take the coastal path and explore the many beaches and creeks in the area.

- ☑ Beach on site
- ☑ Beach within 1 km
- ☑ Sandy beach
- ◯ Blue Flag quality
- ☑ Lifeguard *(high season)*
- ◯ Sun lounger and/or deckchair hire
- ☑ Watersports *(e.g. sailing or windsurfing)*
- ◯ Snacks and drinks
- ◯ Sunshades/sunbeds
- ◯ Dogs allowed *(on the beach)*

Facilities: Two modern, fully equipped toilet blocks kept very clean include washbasins in cubicles, baby baths and facilities for disabled visitors. Laundry facilities. Small shop and bar (24/5-6/9) and takeaway (1/7-31/8). TV room with satellite. Heated outdoor swimming pool (1/5-10/9) with paddling pool, jacuzzi and three slides and a covered, heated pool (19/4-10/9). Tennis. Boules. Play area. In July/Aug organised events and activities for all the family, and a free children's club. Free WiFi. Off site: Attractive sandy beach of Kerleven 10 minutes walk. Golf 800 m. Riding 2 km.

Open: 12 April - 20 September.

Directions: From N165 take D70 Concarneau exit. At first roundabout take D44 (Fouesnant). After 2.5 km. turn right at T-junction, and follow for 2.5 km. and turn left (Port La Forêt). Go over roundabout, (Port La Forêt). After 1 km. turn left (site signed), then in 400 m. turn left to site.

GPS: 47.89923, -3.95505

Charges guide

Per unit incl. 2 persons
and electricity € 16,00 - € 34,00

extra person	€ 7,00 - € 8,50
child (1-7 yrs)	€ 3,00 - € 4,00
dog	€ 2,00 - € 3,00

Facilities: Very clean sanitary blocks include provision for disabled visitors. Washing machines. Motorcaravan service points. Large supermarket, restaurant, takeaway, pizzeria, bar (all open 1/6-15/9). Four outdoor pools with slides and flumes (1/6-19/9). Indoor pool (all season). Fitness room. Massage (Institut de Beauté). Tennis. Play areas. Miniclub, organised entertainment in season. Bicycle hire. WiFi (charged). ATM. Charcoal barbecues are not permitted. Hotel (12 rooms). Off site: Path to the beach 300 m. Fishing and riding. Golf 30 km.

Open: 14 May - 18 September.

Directions: Turn off D101 Hourtin-Soulac road 3 km. north of Hourtin. Then join D101E signed Hourtin-Plage. Site is 300 m. from the beach.

GPS: 45.22297, -1.16465

Charges guide

Per unit incl. 2 persons
and electricity € 28,00 - € 53,00

extra person € 4,00 - € 8,50	
child (3-9 yrs) € 3,00 - € 7,50	
dog € 2,00 - € 6,50	

Airotel Camping de la Côte d'Argent

F-33990 Hourtin-Plage (Gironde)
t: 05 56 09 10 25 e: info@cca33.com
alanrogers.com/FR33110 www.cca33.com

Accommodation: ☑ Pitch ☑ Mobile home/chalet ☑ Hotel/B&B ○ Apartment

Côte d'Argent is a large, well equipped site for leisurely family holidays. It makes an ideal base for walkers and cyclists with over 100 km. of cycle lanes in the area. Hourtin-Plage is a pleasant invigorating resort on the Atlantic coast and a popular location for watersports enthusiasts. The site's top attraction is its pool complex, where wooden bridges connect the pools and islands, and there are sunbathing and play areas plus an indoor heated pool. The site has 600 touring pitches (all with 10A electricity), not always clearly defined, arranged under trees with some on sand. High quality entertainment takes place at the impressive bar/restaurant near the entrance. Spread over 20 hectares of undulating sand-based terrain and in the midst of a pine forest, the site is well organised and ideal for children.

You might like to know

There is direct access from the campsite to a network of 100 km. of cycle tracks. Nearby are the Médoc vineyards, the Arcachon Basin and the Gironde Estuary.

○ Beach on site
☑ Beach within 1 km
☑ Sandy beach
☑ Blue Flag quality
☑ Lifeguard *(high season)*
○ Sun lounger and/or deckchair hire
○ Watersports *(e.g. sailing or windsurfing)*
☑ Snacks and drinks
○ Sunshades/sunbeds
○ Dogs allowed *(on the beach)*

Yelloh! Village le Sérignan-Plage

Le Sérignan Plage, F-34410 Sérignan-Plage (Hérault)
t: 04 67 32 35 33 e: info@leserignanplage.com
alanrogers.com/FR34070 www.yellohvillage.co.uk/camping/le_serignan_plage

Accommodation: ☑ Pitch ☑ Mobile home/chalet ○ Hotel/B&B ○ Apartment

With direct access onto a superb 600 m. sandy beach (including a naturist section) and with three swimming pools, this is a must for a Mediterranean holiday. It is a busy, friendly, family orientated site with a very comprehensive range of amenities. Having recently acquired an adjacent site complete with a small lake, there are now over 1,100 pitches with 278 available for touring units. These vary in size and in terms of shade. They are mainly on sandy soil and all have 6A electricity. The collection of spa pools (balnéo) built in Romanesque style with terracing and columns, overlooked by a very smart restaurant, is still the 'pièce de résistance' and available to use in the afternoons (used by the adjacent naturist site in the mornings). The enthusiastic owners continually surprise us with their unique style and new developments. There are over 300 mobile homes and chalets to let, plus some 400 privately owned units. The heart of the site is a busy and informal area with shops, another good restaurant, an indoor pool and a super roof-top bar. There is a range of sporting activities, children's clubs and evening entertainment – a good holiday choice.

You might like to know

Yelloh! Village Le Serignan Plage has a brilliant aqua complex with a lagoon-style pool covering 850 sq.m, and a special covered pool for very young swimmers.

- ☑ Beach on site
- ○ Beach within 1 km
- ☑ Sandy beach
- ☑ Blue Flag quality
- ○ Lifeguard *(high season)*
- ☑ Sun lounger and/or deckchair hire
- ○ Watersports *(e.g. sailing or windsurfing)*
- ☑ Snacks and drinks
- ☑ Sunshades/sunbeds
- ○ Dogs allowed *(on the beach)*

Facilities: Seven modern blocks of individual design with good facilities including showers with washbasin and WC. Facilities for disabled visitors. Baby bathroom. Launderette. Motorcaravan services. Supermarket, bakery, newsagent and other shops (all season). ATM. Restaurants, bar and takeaway. Hairdresser. Balnéo spa (afternoons). Gym. Heated indoor pool. Outdoor pools (all season). Tennis courts. Multisports courts. Play areas. Trampolines. Children's clubs. Evening entertainment. Sporting activities. Bicycle hire. Bus to Sérignan village (July/Aug). Beach (lifeguards 15/6-15/9). WiFi (charged). Gas barbecues only.
Off site: Fishing 1 km. Riding 1.5 km. Golf 15 km. Sailing and windsurfing school on beach. Local markets.

Open: 26 April - 2 October.

Directions: From A9 exit A75 (Béziers Centre) and exit 64 towards Sérignan, D64 (9 km). Before Sérignan, turn left, Sérignan-Plage (4 km). At small sign (blue) turn right. At T-junction turn left over small road bridge and after left hand bend. Site is 100 m.

GPS: 43.26308, 3.31976

Charges guide

Per unit incl. 2 persons and electricity	€ 15,00 - € 52,00
extra person	€ 5,00 - € 8,50
child (3-7 yrs)	no charge - € 8,50
dog	€ 4,00

Facilities: Good toilet facilities are centrally located and include some washbasins in private cabins, a baby room and ensuite facilities for disabled visitors. Motorcaravan service point. Newly developed fitness and sports area near the beach. In high season beach games, dances, sangria evenings etc, are organised, all aimed particularly towards families along with a small bar/snack bar (high season). Only gas barbecues on pitches. Communal barbecues area. WiFi throughout (charged). Off site: Local market day Tuesday. Bicycle hire and fishing 100 m. Riding 1 km. Boat launching 1.5 km. Golf 2 km. Aqua park at Agde 5 km.

Open: 1 April - 15 October.

Directions: From A9 exit 34 take N312 towards Agde, then N112 towards Sète keeping a lookout for signs to Marseillan-Plage off this road. Site is well signed in Marseillan-Plage.

GPS: 43.3206, 3.5501

Charges guide

Per unit incl. 2 persons and electricity	€ 16,30 - € 33,50
extra person (over 2 yrs)	€ 3,00 - € 6,00
dog	€ 2,00 - € 3,00

France – Marseillan-Plage

Camping la Créole

74 avenue des Campings, F-34340 Marseillan-Plage (Hérault)
t: 04 67 21 92 69 e: campinglacreole@orange.fr
alanrogers.com/FR34220 www.campinglacreole.com

Accommodation: ☑ Pitch ☑ Mobile home/chalet ○ Hotel/B&B ○ Apartment

This is a surprisingly tranquil, well cared for small campsite in the middle of this bustling resort that will appeal to those seeking a rather less frenetic ambience typical of many sites in this area. The Chaput family, who run the site, originally worked the land as a vineyard but developed it into a campsite in 1973. It offers 100 good sized, level, sandy pitches, all with 6A electricity and mostly with shade from mature trees and shrubs. There are also 18 mobile homes available to rent. It benefits from direct access to an extensive sandy beach (secure gated access) and the fact that there is no swimming pool actually contributes to the tranquillity. The beach will be the main attraction here no doubt, and the town's extensive range of bars, restaurants and shops are all within a couple of minutes walk. It is well situated for visiting Sète, a miniature Venice, or Pézenas with an interesting history and lots of art and craft shops. Cap d'Agde, a modern resort with its large marina and super water park for children is popular. If you take a trip on the famous Canal du Midi you may get to see the oyster beds in the Etang de Thau, the inland saltwater lake.

You might like to know

Children can swim safely on the gently sloping beach with its fine sand. There is plenty of shade on the campsite, and all shops and services are less than 100 m. away.

- ☑ Beach on site
- ○ Beach within 1 km
- ☑ Sandy beach
- ☑ Blue Flag quality
- ☑ Lifeguard *(high season)*
- ○ Sun lounger and/or deckchair hire
- ☑ Watersports *(e.g. sailing or windsurfing)*
- ☑ Snacks and drinks
- ○ Sunshades/sunbeds
- ☑ Dogs allowed *(on the beach)*

Facilities: Fully equipped and modern toilet block. Individual toilet units for 56 touring pitches. Baby bath. Facilities for disabled visitors. Laundry. Shop (15/6-15/9). Bar and restaurant (1/5-20/9), takeaway (1/7-31/8). Swimming pool (heated all season). Tennis. Play area. Miniclub and entertainment in high season. WiFi throughout (charged). Bouncy castle (free) Tuesdays and Thursdays. Only electric barbecues permitted. Off site: Beach 300 m. Fishing, boat launching and riding 1 km. Bicycle hire 3 km. Golf 25 km.

Open: 5 April - 27 September.

Directions: From A9 exit 36 (Béziers Ouest) follow directions for Valras-Plage and Vendres-Plage over four roundabouts. At fifth roundabout (Port Conchylicole) follow sign for Vendres-Plage Ouest and site is 500 m. on the left past the Ranch and tourist office. The entrance is quite tight.

GPS: 43.227408, 3.243536

Charges guide

Per unit incl. 2 persons and electricity € 22,00 - € 49,00	
incl. private sanitary facility € 25,00 - € 56,00	
extra person (over 4 yrs) € 5,00 - € 9,00	
dog € 3,00 - € 5,00	

France – Valras-Plage

Camping Blue Bayou

Vendres-Plage Ouest, ave. du Port, F-34350 Valras-Plage (Hérault)
t: 04 67 37 41 97 e: infobluebayou@orange.fr
alanrogers.com/FR34370 www.bluebayou.eu

Accommodation: ☑ Pitch ☑ Mobile home/chalet ○ Hotel/B&B ○ Apartment

The Amiel family have worked hard to make Blue Bayou a comfortable and pleasant place to stay. It is situated at the far end of Vendres-Plage near Le Grau Vendres (the port of Vendres). It is therefore in a much quieter location than many other sites, away from the more hectic, built-up areas of Vendres and Valras-Plage. The beach is 300 m. across sand dunes and there are open views from the site creating a feeling of spaciousness. There are 281 pitches, all with 10A electricity, with 41 privately owned mobile homes and 120 to let, including some chalets. The level grass touring pitches are of a good size, arranged in avenues with shade from tall trees, some with their own sanitary arrangements. The new, larger restaurant and bar area is a focal point, overlooking two swimming pools, one with a toboggan, joined by a bridge where lifeguards station themselves. The owners and their family are very proud of their site and you are made to feel very welcome. The site would make a good choice for couples and families, with a good range of activities and entertainment on offer. In July and August a tourist train runs to link Valras and Vendres.

You might like to know

The site is just 300 m. from one of the most beautiful sandy beaches on the Mediterranean.

- ☑ Beach on site
- ○ Beach within 1 km
- ☑ Sandy beach
- ☑ Blue Flag quality
- ☑ Lifeguard *(high season)*
- ○ Sun lounger and/or deckchair hire
- ☑ Watersports *(e.g. sailing or windsurfing)*
- ☑ Snacks and drinks
- ☑ Sunshades/sunbeds
- ☑ Dogs allowed *(on the beach)*

Facilities: Well equipped, modernised toilet blocks include large showers, some with washbasins. Baby baths and facilities for disabled visitors. Supermarket, bakery and newsagent. Restaurant, bar and takeaway. Swimming pool complex. Entertainment and activity programme with sports, music and cultural activities. Children's club. Beach club. Tennis. Archery. Play areas. Bicycle hire. Electronic games. ATM. Internet access. WiFi throughout (charged). Off site: Village and bicycle hire 100 m. Beach and riding 200 m. Canal du Midi 1 km. Parc Adventure (high wire adventure park) 1.5 km.

Open: April - September.

Directions: From A9 exit 35 (Béziers Est) follow signs for Vias and Agde (N112). After large roundabout pass exit to Cers then take exit for Portiragnes (D37). Follow for 5 km. and pass over Canal du Midi towards Portiragnes-Plage. Site is on left after roundabout.

GPS: 43.28003, 3.36396

Charges guide

Per unit incl. 2 persons and electricity	€ 20,00 - € 52,00
extra person	€ 6,00 - € 10,00
child (under 13 yrs, acc. to age)	no charge - € 10,00
dog	€ 4,00

Camping les Sablons

Avenue des Muriers, F-34420 Portiragnes-Plage (Hérault)
t: 04 67 90 90 55   e: contact@les-sablons.com
alanrogers.com/FR34400   www.les-sablons.com

Accommodation: ☑ Pitch ☑ Mobile home/chalet ○ Hotel/B&B ○ Apartment

Les Sablons is an impressive and popular site with 680 pitches and lots going on, a village in itself. Most of the facilities are arranged around the entrance with shops, a restaurant, a bar and a large pool complex with no less than five slides and three heated pools. There is also direct access to a white sandy beach at the back of the site, close to a small lake. There is good shade on the majority of the site, although some of the newer touring pitches have less shade but are nearer the gate to the beach. On level sandy grass, all 220 touring pitches have 6A electricity. The remainder are taken by a range of mobile homes and chalets, many of which are available for hire. A new entertainment office enables the booking of sporting, cultural and musical activities as well as excursions. Children's clubs, daily activities and evening entertainment are organised. In fact, this is a real holiday venue aiming to keep all the family happy. Some visitors simply stay on the site for their entire holiday – it certainly has everything. The site is very convenient for Béziers airport.

You might like to know

The site has direct access to the beach and dunes (closed 23.00-07.00). There is also a lake with hides for birdwatching.

☑ Beach on site
○ Beach within 1 km
☑ Sandy beach
○ Blue Flag quality
☑ Lifeguard *(high season)*
○ Sun lounger and/or deckchair hire
☑ Watersports *(e.g. sailing or windsurfing)*
☑ Snacks and drinks
○ Sunshades/sunbeds
○ Dogs allowed *(on the beach)*

Facilities: Two large toilet blocks are modern, one very impressive with a special smart nursery unit. Two small ones are more traditional. Facilities for disabled visitors. Laundry. Motorcaravan service point. Supermarket. Smart restaurant (facing stage for entertainment) and bar. Snack bar. Hairdressers. TV room. Play area. Games room. Multisports court. Tennis. Archery. Windsurfing possible from beach. Bicycle hire. Activity programme, children's entertainment, circus school, evening shows and dancing. WiFi (charged). Off site: Riding and fishing 2 km. Golf 15 km. Canal du Midi nearby. Luna Park at Vias. Local markets in Vias (Wed and Sat am), Agde (Thu am) and Beziers (Fri am).

Open: 31 March - 30 September.

Directions: From A9 exit 35 (Béziers Est) follow directions for Agde and Sète on N112. After 4.2 km. turn for Portiragnes. Pass village and continue for 2.5 km. over Canal du Midi then turn left and follow site signs.

GPS: 43.28202, 3.37105

Charges guide

Per unit incl. 2 persons and electricity	€ 16,90 - € 43,80
extra person	€ 3,30 - € 8,10
child (2-10 yrs)	€ 2,20 - € 6,20
dog	€ 1,00 - € 4,10

France – Vias

Camping le Méditerranée Plage

Côte Ouest, F-34450 Vias (Hérault)
t: 04 67 90 99 07 e: contact@mediterranee-plage.com
alanrogers.com/FR34410 www.mediterranee-plage.com

Accommodation: ☑ Pitch ☑ Mobile home/chalet ○ Hotel/B&B ○ Apartment

Set beside the beach in a quiet part of the coast, this site is somewhat different from the majority of beach sites. It has a most impressive entertainment complex situated to one side of the site with very comfortable outdoor seating facing a large stage for entertainment and a very smart bar and restaurant. The colourful furnishings and modern design reflect its Mediterranean setting. The site is very well cared for, with 410 pitches (some 185 used for touring units). Either grassy with a degree of shade or, as you get nearer the beach, more sandy with less shade, all have 6A electricity. The site's other claim to being different is its circus workshop weeks for children (6-12 years) designed to introduce them to the magical world of circus and culminating in a performance for parents each Friday. A new half-board 'country week' includes a dancing course. The pool area and shops – including a bakery and snack bar – are near the entrance which is busy during the day. The site and the white sandy beach are very popular with Dutch and German visitors.

You might like to know

As a change from the beach, a cycle route leads along the Canal du Midi to Béziers with its 13th-century cathedral.

☑ Beach on site
○ Beach within 1 km
☑ Sandy beach
○ Blue Flag quality
○ Lifeguard *(high season)*
○ Sun lounger and/or deckchair hire
○ Watersports *(e.g. sailing or windsurfing)*
☑ Snacks and drinks
○ Sunshades/sunbeds
☑ Dogs allowed *(on the beach)*

Facilities: Four toilet blocks, one heated. One block with fun facilities for children based on Disney characters. Facilities for disabled guests. Laundry facilities. Motorcaravan services. Shops, bar/restaurant, takeaway (16/4-7/9). Swimming pool complex with three pools (all season). Spa, fitness centre and sauna. Play area. Games room. Sports areas. Boules. Tennis. Bicycle hire. Minigolf. Fishing. Riding. Sailing school (15/6-15/9). Communal barbecues. WiFi (charged). Free bus to beach (July-Aug). Off site: Walking and cycle ways in the forest. Atlantic beaches 5 km. Golf 10 km.

Open: 16 April - 21 September.

Directions: Site is off D652 Mimizan-Léon road, 4 km. south of crossroads with D42 at St Girons. The road to the lake and the site is signed at Vielle.

GPS: 43.90285, -1.3125

Charges guide

Per unit incl. 2 persons and electricity	€ 17,40 - € 44,60
extra person	€ 2,20 - € 7,10
child (3-12 yrs)	€ 1,70 - € 6,10
dog	€ 1,20 - € 4,50

France – Vielle-Saint-Girons

Sunêlia le Col-Vert

Lac de Léon, 1548 route de l'Etang, F-40560 Vielle-Saint-Girons (Landes)
t: 08 90 71 00 01   e: contact@colvert.com
alanrogers.com/FR40050   www.colvert.com

Accommodation: ☑ Pitch   ☑ Mobile home/chalet   ○ Hotel/B&B   ○ Apartment

This large, well maintained campsite is well laid out on the shores of Lac de Léon and offers 185 mobile homes for rent and 380 touring pitches. The pitches range from simple ones to those with water and a drain, and there are eight with private, well designed, modern sanitary facilities. In low season it is a quiet site and those pitches beside the lake offer a wonderful backdrop to relaxing pastimes. During the main season it is a lively place for children of all ages. A pool complex offers a standard pool for swimming, a pool for children with a water canon and fountains, plenty of sunbeds and a heated indoor pool. Swimming is also permitted in the lake alongside the many water-based activities. A fitness and beauty spa offers a wide range of treatments. This extensive but natural site edges a nature reserve and stretches along the Lac de Léon, a conservation area, for 1 km. on a narrow frontage. This makes it particularly suitable for those who want to practise watersports such as sailing and windsurfing. Water playground with inflatable games.

You might like to know

Bordering the Lac de Léon and at the heart of a vast nature reserve, le Col Vert was the first French campsite to receive the Ecolabel award. The fine sandy beaches of the Côte d'Argent are nearby.

○ Beach on site
○ Beach within 1 km
☑ Sandy beach
☑ Blue Flag quality
☑ Lifeguard (high season)
○ Sun lounger and/or deckchair hire
☑ Watersports (e.g. sailing or windsurfing)
☑ Snacks and drinks
○ Sunshades/sunbeds
☑ Dogs allowed (on the beach)

Facilities: Four main toilet blocks and two smaller blocks are comfortable and clean with facilities for babies and disabled visitors. Motorcaravan services. Fridge rental. Well stocked shop and bar (all season). Restaurant, takeaway (1/6-8/9). Stage for live shows arranged in July/Aug. Outdoor swimming pool, paddling pool (all season) and heated covered pool (low season). Tennis. Multisports court. Bicycle hire. WiFi (charged). Charcoal barbecues are not permitted. Off site: Riding (July/Aug) 200 m. Surf school 500 m. Beach and fishing 700 m. Golf 18 km.

Open: 18 May - 14 September.

Directions: Turn off D652 at St-Girons on D42 towards St-Girons-Plage. Site is on left before coming to beach (4.5 km).

GPS: 43.95166, -1.35212

Charges guide

Per unit incl. 2 persons and electricity € 19,00 - € 37,00
extra person (over 5 yrs) € 6,00
dog € 4,00

France – Vielle-Saint-Girons

Camping Club International Eurosol

Route de la Plage, F-40560 Vielle-Saint-Girons (Landes)
t: 05 58 47 90 14 e: contact@camping-eurosol.com
alanrogers.com/FR40060 www.camping-eurosol.com

Accommodation: ☑ Pitch ☑ Mobile home/chalet ○ Hotel/B&B ○ Apartment

Eurosol is an attractive, friendly and well maintained site extending over 15 hectares of undulating ground amongst mature pine trees giving good shade. Of the 356 touring pitches, 231 have electricity (10A) with 120 fully serviced. A wide range of mobile homes and chalets are available for rent too. This is very much a family site with multi-lingual entertainers. Many games and tournaments are organised and a beach volleyball competition is held regularly in front of the bar. The adjacent boules terrain is floodlit. An excellent sandy beach 700 metres from the site has supervised bathing in high season and is ideal for surfing. The landscaped swimming pool complex is impressive with three large pools, one of which is covered and heated, and a large children's paddling pool. There is a convivial restaurant and takeaway food service. A large supermarket is well stocked with fresh bread daily and international newspapers. A number of cycle trails lead from the site through the vast forests of Les Landes, and a riding centre is located just 100 m. away.

You might like to know

A quiet, very high quality camping village in the shade of the pine forest, and a great spot for unforgettable family holidays.

○ Beach on site
☑ Beach within 1 km
☑ Sandy beach
○ Blue Flag quality
☑ Lifeguard *(high season)*
○ Sun lounger and/or deckchair hire
○ Watersports *(e.g. sailing or windsurfing)*
☑ Snacks and drinks
☑ Sunshades/sunbeds
☑ Dogs allowed *(on the beach)*

Facilities: Five toilet blocks (opened as required) are well maintained with showers and many washbasins in cabins. Facilities for babies, children and disabled visitors. Laundry facilities. Motorcaravan services. Fridge hire. Shop (freshly baked bread) and bar (4/5-19/9). Restaurant, snack bar, pizzas and takeaway (4/5-19/9). Covered pool and outdoor pools. Minigolf. Tennis. Bicycle hire. Play area. Entertainment and activities (high season). Gas or electric barbecues only. WiFi (charged). Off site: Beach and fishing 500 m. Bus service and riding 1 km. Golf 8 km. Mimizan 8 km.

Open: 4 May - 20 September.

Directions: Heading west from Mimizan centre, take D626 passing Abbey Museum. Straight on at lights (crossing D87/D67), at next lights turn left. After 2 km. at T-junction turn left. Follow signs to site.

GPS: 44.20447, -1.29099

Charges guide

Per unit incl. 3 persons and electricity	€ 18,00 - € 52,00
extra person	€ 4,00 - € 10,00
child (4-12 yrs)	€ 3,00 - € 8,00
dog	€ 3,00 - € 5,00

France – Mimizan-Plage

Airotel Club Marina-Landes

Rue Marina, F-40200 Mimizan (Landes)
t: 05 58 09 12 66   e: contact@clubmarina.com
alanrogers.com/FR40080   www.marinalandes.com

Accommodation: ☑ Pitch   ☑ Mobile home/chalet   ○ Hotel/B&B   ☑ Apartment

Well maintained and clean, with helpful staff, Club Marina-Landes would be a very good choice for a family holiday. Activities include discos, play groups for children, specially trained staff to entertain teenagers and concerts for more mature campers. There are numerous sports opportunities and a superb sandy beach nearby. A nightly curfew ensures that all have a good night's sleep. A new leisure pool is planned. The site has 356 touring pitches (316 with 10A electricity) and 147 mobile homes and chalets for rent. The pitches are on firm grass, most with hedges and they are large (mostly 100 sq.m. or larger). If ever a campsite could be said to have two separate identities, then Club Marina-Landes is surely the one. In early and late season it is quiet, with the pace of life in low gear – come July until 1 September, all the facilities are open and there is fun for all the family with the chance that family members will only meet together at meal times.

You might like to know

Why not take the Mailloueyre lake trail (1 km, 15 minutes on foot)? The area is officially classified as a nature reserve and is a delight for botanists and nature lovers alike.

○ Beach on site
☑ Beach within 1 km
☑ Sandy beach
○ Blue Flag quality
☑ Lifeguard *(high season)*
○ Sun lounger and/or deckchair hire
☑ Watersports *(e.g. sailing or windsurfing)*
☑ Snacks and drinks
○ Sunshades/sunbeds
☑ Dogs allowed *(on the beach)*

Facilities: Sanitary facilities include free showers, provision for disabled visitors, and laundry facilites. Heated outdoor pool (24/5-21/9), new indoor pool in 2014, small supermarket, renovated bar/restaurant/takeaway with themed meals in high season, (all open all season). Children's play area. Kids' Clubs (3-11 yrs) and new 'Salle d'Animation' with full programme of activities and entertainment (July/Aug). Multisports court. Beach volleyball and beach soccer. Outdoor fitness equipment. Bicycle hire. WiFi. Communal barbecue. Off site: Beach 700 m. Surf school, rafting, canoeing and kayaking, quad biking, riding, children's farm, minigolf and even Pelote Basque. Biarritz 18 km. Spain 50 km.

Open: 12 April - 21 September.

Directions: Labenne-Océan is 4 km. west of Labenne. From north on A85 leave at exit 8 and take D28 east, then turn south on D810 to Labenne. In Labenne turn west on D126 Avenue de l'Océan. Site is on right in 3 km. immediately after crossing river.

GPS: 43.59634, -1.46136

Charges guide

Per unit incl. 2 persons and electricity	€ 15,00 - € 40,00
extra person	€ 4,00 - € 8,00
child (2-12 yrs)	€ 3,00 - € 5,00
dog	€ 2,00 - € 5,00

France – Labenne-Océan

Camping le Boudigau

45 avenue de l'Ocean, F-40530 Labenne-Océan (Landes)
t: 02 51 20 41 94 e: contact@camp-atlantique.com
alanrogers.com/FR40540 www.boudigau.com

Accommodation: ☑ Pitch ☑ Mobile home/chalet ○ Hotel/B&B ○ Apartment

Taking its name from a little river that runs alongside, and situated just a kilometre from the extensive beach at Labenne-Océan, le Boudigeau is a well equipped site that becomes very lively in high season. There are 301 pitches, of which 32 are for tourers, all with electricity (6A), and numerous trees providing plenty of shade; rental chalets and mobile homes occupy the remaining pitches. In July and August, the site is very much geared to children and young people, with Kids' Clubs for ages 3-11 years, and a full programme of sporting activities and entertainment for the whole family. Labenne-Océan is at the southern end of the rugged coastline of Les Landes, just a few kilometres north of the fashionable resort of Biarritz; to the south is the Basque Region and beyond that, Spain. As a result, the options for excursions are numerous, whether you drive out into the countryside to explore the picturesque villages or head for Bayonne, Biarritz, Saint Jean-de-Luz, Saint Jean Pied-de-Port, Dax or Capbreton.

You might like to know

A most friendly, family campsite, just 500 m. from the beach.

○ Beach on site
☑ Beach within 1 km
☑ Sandy beach
○ Blue Flag quality
☑ Lifeguard *(high season)*
○ Sun lounger and/or deckchair hire
☑ Watersports *(e.g. sailing or windsurfing)*
☑ Snacks and drinks
☑ Sunshades/sunbeds
☑ Dogs allowed *(on the beach)*

Facilities: Three good clean toilet blocks have washbasins in cabins and mainly British style toilets. Facilities for disabled visitors. Baby baths. Motorcaravan service point. Shop with gas. New bar/restaurant complex with entertainment. Swimming pool complex (supervised July/Aug). Games room. Play area. Tennis. Bicycle hire. Boules. Archery. Fishing. Water skiing. Watersports equipment hire. Tournaments (June-Aug). Skateboard park. Trampolines. Miniclub. No charcoal barbecues on pitches. Communal barbecue area. WiFi (charged). Off site: Riding 2 km. Golf 12 km. Beach 17 km.

Open: 6 April - 8 September.

Directions: Take D652 from Sanguinet to Biscarrosse and site is signed on the right in 6 km. Turn right and follow tarmac road for 2 km.

GPS: 44.46052, -1.13065

Charges guide

Per unit incl. 2 persons
and electricity € 26,50 - € 54,00

extra person € 3,60 - € 10,00

child (3-7 yrs) € 3,60 - € 8,20

dog € 6,20 - € 8,20

France – Biscarrosse

Camping Resort la Rive

Route de Bordeaux, F-40600 Biscarrosse (Landes)
t: 05 58 78 12 33 e: info@larive.fr
alanrogers.com/FR40100 www.larive.fr

Accommodation: ☑ Pitch ☑ Mobile home/chalet ○ Hotel/B&B ○ Apartment

Surrounded by pine woods, la Rive has a superb beach-side location on Lac de Sanguinet. With a total of 800 pitches, it provides 250 mostly level, numbered and clearly defined touring pitches of 100 sq.m. all with electricity connections (10A). The swimming pool complex is wonderful with pools linked by water channels and bridges. There is also a jacuzzi, paddling pool and two large swimming pools all surrounded by sunbathing areas and decorated with palm trees. An indoor pool is heated and open all season. This is a friendly site with a good mix of nationalities. The latest additions are a super children's aquapark with various games, and a top quality bar/restaurant complex where regular entertainment is organised. There are plans to extend the outdoor pools with the addition of new slides more than 200 m. long. The beach is excellent, shelving gently to provide safe bathing for all ages. There are windsurfers and small craft can be launched from the site's slipway.

You might like to know

The fine sandy beach can be accessed from the campsite, and there is a wide range of watersports for the whole family.

☑ Beach on site
○ Beach within 1 km
☑ Sandy beach
○ Blue Flag quality
○ Lifeguard *(high season)*
○ Sun lounger and/or deckchair hire
☑ Watersports *(e.g. sailing or windsurfing)*
○ Snacks and drinks
○ Sunshades/sunbeds
○ Dogs allowed *(on the beach)*

Facilities: Nine well appointed, recently renovated toilet blocks with facilities for disabled visitors. Motorcaravan services. Well stocked supermarket and various smaller shops in high season. Several restaurants, takeaway and three bars (all open all season). Large pool complex (no Bermuda shorts; open all season) including new covered pool and Polynesian themed bar. Tennis. Multisports pitch. Minigolf. Outdoor fitness area. Fishing. Bicycle hire. Riding centre. Organised activities including frequent discos and karaoke evenings (29/3-12/9). Spa, massages and beauty area. Only communal barbecues are allowed. WiFi over site (charged). Off site: Beach 400 m. Sailing 2 km. Golf 8 km.

Open: 29 March - 28 September.

Directions: Leave RN10 at Magescq exit heading for Soustons. Pass through Soustons following signs for Vieux-Boucau. Bypass this town and site is clearly signed to the left at second roundabout.

GPS: 43.79778, -1.40111

Charges guide

Per unit incl. 2 persons and electricity € 21,55 - € 61,80	
extra person € 4,85 - € 9,10	
child (under 13 yrs) € 3,85 - € 6,25	
dog € 3,10 - € 5,85	

France – Messanges

Airotel le Vieux Port

Plage Sud, F-40660 Messanges (Landes)
t: 01 76 76 70 00   e: contact@levieuxport.com
alanrogers.com/FR40180   www.levieuxport.com

Accommodation: ☑ Pitch   ☑ Mobile home/chalet   ○ Hotel/B&B   ○ Apartment

A well established destination appealing particularly to families with teenage children, this lively site has 1,546 pitches (975 for touring) of mixed sizes, most with electricity (6A). The camping area is well shaded by pines and pitches are generally of a good size, attractively grouped around the toilet blocks. There are many tour operators here and well over a third of the site is taken up with mobile homes and chalets. An enormous 7,000 sq.m. aquatic park is now open, and is the largest on any French campsite. This heated complex is exceptional, boasting five outdoor pools (all 25ºC), three large water slides plus waves and a heated spa. There is also a heated indoor pool. The area to the north of Bayonne is heavily forested and a number of very large campsites are attractively located close to the superb Atlantic beaches. Le Vieux Port is probably the largest, and certainly one of the most impressive, of these. At the back of the site a path leads across the dunes to a good beach (400 m). All in all, this is a lively site with a great deal to offer an active family.

You might like to know

The whole family will love the enormous sandy beach, just five minutes away and accessed directly from the site.

○ Beach on site
☑ Beach within 1 km
☑ Sandy beach
○ Blue Flag quality
☑ Lifeguard *(high season)*
○ Sun lounger and/or deckchair hire
☑ Watersports *(e.g. sailing or windsurfing)*
☑ Snacks and drinks
○ Sunshades/sunbeds
○ Dogs allowed *(on the beach)*

Facilities: Seven toilet blocks of a high standard and very well maintained, have washbasins in cabins, large showers, baby rooms and facilities for disabled visitors. Motorcaravan service point. Washing machines and dryers. Fridge rental. Supermarket. Bars, restaurants and takeaways. Indoor pool, jacuzzi and sauna (charged July/Aug). Outdoor pool area with jacuzzi and paddling pool (15/6-15/9). Multisport pitch. Play area. Bicycle hire. Beach access. Internet access. Electric barbecues only. Off site: Fishing and beach 300 m. Golf and tennis 700 m. Sailing 6 km. Riding 8 km.

Open: Easter - 1 November.

Directions: From the N10 take D142 to Lèon, then D652 to Moliets-et-Mar. Follow signs to Moliets-Plage, site is well signed.

GPS: 43.85242, -1.38732

Charges guide

Per unit incl. 2 persons and electricity € 22,70 - € 48,60	
extra person € 6,00 - € 8,50	
child (under 13 yrs) € 4,00 - € 6,00	
dog no charge - € 5,00	

Prices are for reserved pitches.

France – Moliets-Plage

Le Saint-Martin Camping

Avenue de l'Océan, F-40660 Moliets-Plage (Landes)
t: 05 58 48 52 30 e: contact@camping-saint-martin.fr
alanrogers.com/FR40190 www.camping-saint-martin.fr

Accommodation: ☑ Pitch ☑ Mobile home/chalet ○ Hotel/B&B ○ Apartment

A family site aimed mainly at couples and young families, le Saint-Martin is a welcome change from most of the sites in this area in that it has only a relatively small number of mobile homes (127) compared to the number of touring pitches (383). First impressions are of a neat, tidy, well cared for site and the direct access to a wonderful fine sandy beach is an added bonus. The pitches are mainly typically French in style with low hedges separating them, and with some shade. Electricity hook ups are 10/15A and a number of pitches also have water and drainage. Entertainment in high season is low key (with the emphasis on quiet nights) – daytime competitions and a miniclub, plus the occasional evening entertainment, well away from the pitches and with no discos or karaoke. With pleasant chalets and mobile homes to rent, a top-class pool complex and an 18-hole golf course 700 m. away (special rates negotiated), this would be an ideal destination for a golfing weekend or longer stay.

You might like to know

Courant d'Huchet, a conservation area, is delightful and has a number of walks and some beautiful views.

- ☑ Beach on site
- ○ Beach within 1 km
- ☑ Sandy beach
- ○ Blue Flag quality
- ☑ Lifeguard *(high season)*
- ○ Sun lounger and/or deckchair hire
- ○ Watersports *(e.g. sailing or windsurfing)*
- ○ Snacks and drinks
- ○ Sunshades/sunbeds
- ☑ Dogs allowed *(on the beach)*

Kawan Village le Grand Large

F-50340 Les Pieux (Manche)
t: 02 33 52 40 75 e: info@legrandlarge.com
alanrogers.com/FR50060 www.legrandlarge.com

Accommodation: ☑ Pitch ☑ Mobile home/chalet ○ Hotel/B&B ○ Apartment

Le Grand Large is a well established, quality family site with direct access to a long sandy beach and within a 20 km. drive of Cherbourg. It is a neat and tidy site with 119 touring pitches divided and separated by hedging giving an orderly, well laid out and attractive appearance. Almost all have electricity (10A Europlug), water and drainage. There are 49 mobile homes for rent in three separate areas. The reception area is at the entrance (with a security barrier) and the forecourt is decorated with flower beds. To the rear of the site and laid out in the sandhills is an excellent play area. Not surprisingly the sandy beach is the big attraction. The length of units is restricted to eight metres to prevent any problems accessing pitches. Roads around the site are tarmac and many of the plants and shrubs that you see bordering these carry name tags in four languages. The pleasant views from the site stretch across the bay to the tip of the Cherbourg peninsula. Every effort is made to attract and cater for families with young children, so noisy entertainment is not an option.

You might like to know

Le Grand Large Les Pieux is on a gently sloping sandy beach facing the Channel Islands, and just 20 minutes from Cherbourg. Visit Cité de la Mer or have a day out on Jersey or Guernsey.

- ☑ Beach on site
- ○ Beach within 1 km
- ☑ Sandy beach
- ☑ Blue Flag quality
- ○ Lifeguard *(high season)*
- ○ Sun lounger and/or deckchair hire
- ○ Watersports *(e.g. sailing or windsurfing)*
- ☑ Snacks and drinks
- ○ Sunshades/sunbeds
- ☑ Dogs allowed *(on the beach)*

Facilities: Two well maintained toilet blocks. The main one is modern and includes washbasins in cubicles and some family rooms. There are some showers and WCs to the outside of the building. Provision for disabled visitors. Baby bathroom. Laundry area. Motorcaravan services. Shop for basics, bar (all season). Restaurant and takeaway (6/7-30/8). Heated swimming and paddling pools (indoor all season, outdoor 15/6-1/9). Play area. Tennis. Boules. Fishing. TV room. Some entertainment (July/Aug). WiFi over site (charged).
Off site: Bicycle hire and riding 5 km. Golf 15 km. Two supermarkets in Les Pieux. Day trips by ferry to the Channel Islands (May-Sept) from nearby Diellete.

Open: 13 April - 22 September.

Directions: From Cherbourg port take N13 south for 2 km. Branch right on D650 (previously D904) signed Carteret. Continue for 18 km. to Les Pieux. Take D4 in town and turn left just after 'Super U' supermarket. Follow site signs via D117/517.
GPS: 49.49452, -1.84246

Charges guide

Per unit incl. 2 persons and electricity	€ 21,00 - € 37,00
extra person	€ 4,50 - € 8,00
child (3-10 yrs)	€ 3,00 - € 4,00
dog (max. 1)	no charge

Facilities: Toilet blocks (one heated) have free hot water, washbasins in cubicles, baby baths and facilities for children and disabled visitors. Laundry facilities. Swimming pool with water slides. Play areas including ball pool. Tennis. TV. Entertainment programme in high season for all ages. Bicycle hire. Canoe hire. Beach. Guided tours. Internet access and WiFi (charged). Communal barbecue areas (gas or electric only on pitches). Off site: Fishing 50 m. Shop with bakery. Bar, restaurant, crêperie, takeaway all 200 m. Sailing 1.5 km. Riding 3.5 km. Golf 13 km.

Open: 27 April - 15 September.

Directions: From N165 at Auray take D28 (La Trinité-sur-Mer). On through town following signs to Carnac-Plage on D186. Site signed off this road to the south. Take care to take road signed to Kervillen Plage where it forks. At seafront turn right. Site is 300 m. on right. The site is well signed.

GPS: 47.57563, -3.02890

Charges guide

Per unit incl. 2 persons and electricity (10A)	€ 22,60 - € 43,30
extra person	€ 5,20
child (2-17 yrs)	€ 2,00 - € 4,20
dog no charge	- € 1,30

Camping de la Plage

Plage de Kervillen, F-56470 La Trinité-sur-Mer (Morbihan)
t: 02 97 55 73 28   e: camping@camping-plage.com
alanrogers.com/FR56020   www.camping-plage.com

Accommodation: ☑ Pitch ☑ Mobile home/chalet ○ Hotel/B&B ○ Apartment

The Carnac and La Trinité area of Brittany is popular with British holidaymakers. Camping de la Plage is a well established site with direct access to the safe, sandy beach of Kervillen Plage. There are 195 grass pitches, some of which are used by tour operators and others occupied by mobile homes (available to rent), but many are available for touring. Pitches are all hedged and of a good size (100 sq.m) and have 6/10A electricity, water and drainage. The site has a slight slope and a few pitches reflect this. With narrow roads and sharp bends, la Plage may not be suitable for larger units. The shop, restaurant and bar, 200 m. along the coast, and overlooking Quiberon Bay, are used by local residents and provide excellent value. The restaurant and takeaway have extensive menus. A lively entertainment programme for all ages in high season makes this an attractive site for family holidays. La Trinité is a world famous yachting centre and is a delightful place for an evening stroll. It also hosts a colourful market on Tuesdays and Thursdays.

You might like to know

There is a choice of beaches along the coast, some where dogs are allowed, some where you can practise watersports.

☑ Beach on site
○ Beach within 1 km
☑ Sandy beach
○ Blue Flag quality
☑ Lifeguard (high season)
○ Sun lounger and/or deckchair hire
○ Watersports (e.g. sailing or windsurfing)
☑ Snacks and drinks
○ Sunshades/sunbeds
☑ Dogs allowed (on the beach)

France – Carnac

Camping les Menhirs

Allée Saint-Michel, F-56340 Carnac (Morbihan)
t: 02 97 52 94 67   e: contact@lesmenhirs.com
alanrogers.com/FR56270   www.lesmenhirs.com

Accommodation: ☑ Pitch ☑ Mobile home/chalet ○ Hotel/B&B ○ Apartment

Facilities: Three spotless, modern, light toilet blocks with washbasins in cabins, facilities for children, babies and disabled campers. A further en-suite unit for disabled visitors is by the pool complex. Laundry. Shop. Comfortable bar with satellite TV and takeaway (26/5-16/9). Heated indoor (19/4-15/9) and outdoor swimming pools (1/5-20/9), the latter with slides. Fitness complex with massage, multi-gym, jacuzzi, sauna and solarium. Multisports pitch. Tennis. Boules. Play areas. Children's club and evening entertainment (July/Aug). WiFi throughout (charged). Accommodation for rent. Off site: Beach 300 m. Bicycle hire 500 m. Minigolf 800 m. Sailing 1 km. Town centre 1 km. Bars and restaurants within easy walking distance. Golf 15 km.

Open: 19 April - 20 September.

Directions: From Auray take D786 to Carnac and Quiberon. After 5 km. turn south on D119 towards Carnac at roundabout. 600 m. beyond next roundabout fork left, (La Trinité-sur-Mer, Plages). Straight on at lights. Fork left at first roundabout. Turn left at next roundabout (T-junction) and site is signed at 250 m. on left.

GPS: 47.57653, -3.06890

Charges guide

Per unit incl. 2 persons and electricity	€ 27,85 - € 51,35
extra person	€ 4,15 - € 8,30
child (2-6 yrs)	€ 3,10 - € 6,15

Although located within the built-up area of the popular resort of Carnac, and only 300 m. from the beach, this campsite feels much more rural. Catering for all ages, this is a friendly site and lively in high season with plenty of activities including evening entertainment and a club for children. There are 350 pitches; 164 touring pitches and the remainder used for mobile homes and chalets, of which the majority are used by tour operators. The touring pitches are in groups and are large, level and hedged. Nineteen pitches are designated Luxe, being quite large (110-120 sq.m), and six are Privilege (115-130 sq.m. including barbecue). All have electricity (10A), water and drainage. The central complex, containing the pools and games areas, all overlooked by the bar and its terrace, makes a convivial focal point. The town and seafront can be explored on foot and the Brittany coast and the Gulf of Morbihan are within easy reach by car or bicycle. American motorhomes should book ahead.

You might like to know

Low season discounts on pitches:
5% reduction for a 7-night stay;
8% discount for a 14-night stay.

○ Beach on site
☑ Beach within 1 km
☑ Sandy beach
○ Blue Flag quality
☑ Lifeguard *(high season)*
○ Sun lounger and/or deckchair hire
○ Watersports *(e.g. sailing or windsurfing)*
☑ Snacks and drinks
☑ Sunshades/sunbeds
☑ Dogs allowed *(on the beach)*

France – Quiberon

Camping Do Mi Si La Mi

31 rue de la Vierge, Saint Julien-Plage, F-56170 Quiberon (Morbihan)
t: 02 97 50 22 52   e: camping@domisilami.com
alanrogers.com/FR56360   www.domisilami.com

Accommodation: ☑ Pitch ☑ Mobile home/chalet ○ Hotel/B&B ○ Apartment

Facilities: Six sanitary blocks (one for families), with good hot showers. Separate laundry. Shop. Bar. TV room. Bouncy castles. Multisport courts. Children's club. WiFi throughout (charged). Off site: Bar, restaurant, supermarket 50 m. Beaches and bicycle hire 100 m. Town centre 2 km. Golf and riding 3 km.

Open: 1 April - 2 November.

Directions: From N165 Vannes-Lorient dual carriageway south of Auray, take Carnac/Ploemel exit. Continue southwest on D768 through the town of Plouharmel following signs for Quiberon. 25 km. from the N165 but before reaching Quiberon, the site is signed to the left at St Julien-Plage.
GPS: 47.49974, -3.12026

Charges guide

Per unit incl. 2 persons and electricity	€ 16,30 - € 26,30
extra person	€ 2,80 - € 5,00
child (under 7 yrs)	€ 2,10 - € 3,00
dog	€ 2,00 - € 2,50

Occupying a five-hectare site on the Quiberon Peninsula, just 100 metres from the sandy beaches, this campsite has plenty to offer and is particularly quiet and laid back in low season. Of the 350 pitches, 189 are for touring and are set amongst high mature hedges giving plenty of shade and privacy; some have sea views. Long leads are required on a few pitches as hook-ups can be shared between three or four pitches. The excellent facilities for children are in a well fenced area and include climbing frames, bouncy castles and multisports courts. Treasure hunts and other activities are organised daily in high season. Well managed reception on the opposite side of the road to the campsite. This site is ideally situated for exploring this fascinating area.

You might like to know

Entertainment includes over 15 games, inflatables, a multisports area, pétanque and table tennis. WiFi is available over the whole site.

○ Beach on site
☑ Beach within 1 km
☑ Sandy beach
○ Blue Flag quality
○ Lifeguard (high season)
○ Sun lounger and/or deckchair hire
○ Watersports (e.g. sailing or windsurfing)
☑ Snacks and drinks
○ Sunshades/sunbeds
○ Dogs allowed (on the beach)

Facilities: Good quality toilet blocks with baby baths and two units for disabled visitors. Washing facilities (only two open at night). Washing machines, dryers. Motorcaravan services. Shop (including gas), restaurant and takeaway, bar, heated swimming and paddling pools, wellness facilities, fitness room (all open all season). Playground. General room, TV room, games room, films. Fishing. Surf school. Dogs are not accepted. WiFi (charged). Off site: Golf 500 m. Bicycle hire 2 km. Riding 3 km. Sailing 5 km. New oceanographic centre at Biarritz.

Open: 15 May - 30 September.

Directions: From A63 exit 4, take the N10 south towards Bidart. At roundabout after the Intermarché supermarket turn right (signed for Biarritz). After 600 m. turn left at site sign.

GPS: 43.45458, -1.57649

Charges guide

Per unit incl. 2 persons, electricity and water € 32,00 - € 56,00	
tent pitch € 26,00 - € 46,00	
extra person (over 4 yrs) € 8,00 - € 13,00	

France – Bidart

Camping le Pavillon Royal

Avenue du Prince de Galles, F-64210 Bidart (Pyrénées-Atlantiques)
t: 05 59 23 00 54   e: info@pavillon-royal.com
alanrogers.com/FR64060   www.pavillon-royal.com

Accommodation: ☑ Pitch ☑ Mobile home/chalet ○ Hotel/B&B ○ Apartment

Le Pavillon Royal has an excellent situation on raised ground overlooking the sea (100 m. from the beach), with good views along the coast to the south and to the north coast of Spain beyond. There is a large heated swimming pool and sunbathing area in the centre of the site. The camping area is divided up into 325 marked, level pitches, many of a good size. Seventy five are reserved for tents and are only accessible on foot. The remainder are connected by asphalt roads. All have electricity. Much of the campsite is in full sun, although the area for tents is shaded. Beneath the site – and only a very short walk down – stretches a wide sandy beach where the Atlantic rollers provide ideal conditions for surfing. A central, marked out section of the beach is supervised by lifeguards (from mid June). There is also a section with rocks and pools. Reservation in high season is advisable.

You might like to know

The only campsite in the Basque country with direct access to the beach, where there is a surf school. The site also has a solar-heated swimming pool.

○ Beach on site
☑ Beach within 1 km
☑ Sandy beach
○ Blue Flag quality
☑ Lifeguard *(high season)*
○ Sun lounger and/or deckchair hire
☑ Watersports *(e.g. sailing or windsurfing)*
☑ Snacks and drinks
☑ Sunshades/sunbeds
○ Dogs allowed *(on the beach)*

Facilities:
Large modern toilet block, fully equipped and with some washbasins in cabins. Baby bath. Some facilities for disabled visitors. Washing machines. Shop, bar, restaurant and takeaway (all season). Heated swimming pool (May-Sept). Entertainment in high season. Play area. Bicycle hire. WiFi throughout (charged). Path to beach. Only gas barbecues permitted. Max. 1 dog per pitch. Off site: Tourist train in high season. Aquatic park, adventure park, karting, riding and minigolf all within walking distance.

Open: 12 April - 27 September.

Directions: From A9 take exit 42 (Perpignan-Sud) and follow N114 for Argelès. At exit 10 follow directions for Taxo d'Avall then Plage Nord. Site is clearly signed off coast road in the St Cyprien direction.

GPS: 42.580606, 3.032854

Charges guide

Per unit incl. 2 persons and electricity	€ 22,00 - € 40,00
extra person	€ 5,00 - € 9,00
child (0-10 yrs)	no charge - € 6,00
dog	€ 5,00

France – Argelès-sur-Mer

MS Vacances Camping Club Le Littoral

Route du Littoral, F-66700 Argelès-sur-Mer (Pyrénées-Orientales)
t: 02 53 81 70 00 e: reservation@ms-vacances.com
alanrogers.com/FR66060 www.ms-vacances.com

Accommodation: ☑ Pitch ☑ Mobile home/chalet ○ Hotel/B&B ○ Apartment

Sites with access to the beach are difficult to find and, even though le Littoral is not directly beside the beach, it is only 800 metres away by footpath. It offers much accommodation in mobile homes as well as 51 good sized, level touring pitches with shade and 6A electricity. An attractive pool area is open from May to September. Argelès is a very popular holiday resort with good sandy beaches. The border with Spain is only 30 km. away. The site is situated on the north side of Argelès, between the coast road and the beach, so access is good, although there could be some road noise in high season. The site has been taken over by a new group, Camp'Atlantic and is looking smart with a new reception and tarmac roadways. However, there are now fewer touring pitches and the emphasis is on mobile homes with over 127 to let and 105 privately owned. The site is well looked after and the pool area is particularly welcoming.

You might like to know

Les Déferlantes music festival at Argelès-sur-Mer and the Fêtes de la Saint Vincent at Collioure are not to be missed, and the Abbey at Saint Martin du Canigou is worth the climb.

○ Beach on site
☑ Beach within 1 km
☑ Sandy beach
☑ Blue Flag quality
○ Lifeguard *(high season)*
○ Sun lounger and/or deckchair hire
☑ Watersports *(e.g. sailing or windsurfing)*
☑ Snacks and drinks
☑ Sunshades/sunbeds
☑ Dogs allowed *(on the beach)*

Facilities: Nine well equipped sanitary blocks are well placed around the site. Facilities for babies. Laundry. Motorcaravan service point. Shops, bars, restaurant and takeaway all open when site is open. Swimming pools with lifeguards, jacuzzi and solarium. Fitness club. Children's clubs. Artistic workshops (pottery, crafts etc). Daily sports and entertainment programme. Day trips. Evening entertainment with cabaret. Disco. Communal barbecue. Sailing club. Beach club. Tennis. Bicycle hire. Play areas. WiFi. Direct access to beach. Off site: Riding nearby. Rafting, canoeing and quad bike treks by arrangement. Canet 500 m. with tourist train in high season. Perpignan 10 km. Collioure, Port Vendres and the Spanish border.

Open: 26 April - 13 September.

Directions: Take exit 41 from A9 autoroute and follow signs for Canet. On outskirts of town follow signs for St Cyprien/Plage Sud. Site is very clearly signed on southern edge of Canet Plage.
GPS: 42.6757, 3.03135

Charges guide

Per unit incl. 2 persons and electricity	€ 24,20 - € 50,20
extra person	€ 8,00 - € 15,00
child (0-5 yrs)	no charge - € 7,50
dog	no charge - € 4,50

Camping Mar Estang

Route de Saint Cyprien, F-66140 Canet-en-Roussillon (Pyrénées-Orientales)
t: 04 68 80 35 53   e: contactme@marestang.com
alanrogers.com/FR66090   www.marestang.com

Accommodation: ☑ Pitch ☑ Mobile home/chalet ○ Hotel/B&B ○ Apartment

Le Mar Estang is a large, impressive, 'all singing, all dancing' site with something for everyone. Situated on the edge of Canet, between the Etang (part of the Réserve Naturelle de Canet/St Nazaire) and the sea, there is access to the sandy beach from the site by two tunnels under the road. If you don't fancy the beach, the site has not one but two attractive pool complexes linked by a bridge. They are amazing, providing slides, toboggans, jacuzzi, paddling pool and a heated pool, all with lifeguards. You can swim seriously, learn to swim or scuba dive, or just enjoy the fun pools. Who needs the beach! There are 600 pitches in total, some 300 for touring units, with 6A electricity, and some degree of shade, on sandy ground. The rest are used by tour operators or have site-owned mobile homes to rent. A very wide range of activities and entertainment is organised all season, with children's clubs in high season and a beach club for watersports. Children and teenagers would have a great time here and parents would enjoy Canet-Plage with its shops and restaurants.

You might like to know

The campsite is situated between a beautiful sandy beach and a nature reserve, in France's sunniest region.

☑ Beach on site
○ Beach within 1 km
☑ Sandy beach
○ Blue Flag quality
☑ Lifeguard *(high season)*
○ Sun lounger and/or deckchair hire
○ Watersports *(e.g. sailing or windsurfing)*
○ Snacks and drinks
○ Sunshades/sunbeds
☑ Dogs allowed *(on the beach)*

Facilities: Three modern toilet blocks include facilities for babies and disabled visitors. Bar, restaurant and takeaway (1/7-31/8). Swimming and paddling pools (all season). TV. Play Area. Some evening entertainment in high season. Max. one dog. Only gas barbecues allowed. WiFi throughout. Off site: Beach 300 m. Boat launching 500 m. Riding 1 km.

Open: 12 April - 21 September.

Directions: From A9 take exit 41 and follow signs towards Canet via the D83 and D81 until a roundabout signed Ste Marie-la-Mer Plage. Turn left into Ste Marie-Plage and follow campsite signs.
GPS: 42.72671, 3.03293

Charges guide

Per unit incl. 2 persons and electricity € 18,00 - € 38,00	
extra person € 5,00 - € 9,00	
child (0-4 yrs) € 6,00	
dog € 5,00	

No credit cards.

France – Sainte Marie-la-Mer

Camping la Pergola

21 avenue Frederic Mistral, F-66478 Sainte Marie-la-Mer (Pyrénées-Orientales)
t: 02 51 20 41 94 e: contact@camp-atlantique.com
alanrogers.com/FR66100 www.camp-atlantique.com

Accommodation: ☑ Pitch ☑ Mobile home/chalet ○ Hotel/B&B ○ Apartment

La Pergola is an attractive tranquil campsite with 183 pitches which include 98 for tourers, all with 10A electricity. It is located in a mainly residential area of this up-and-coming and, at times, quite lively, seaside resort. Family-run, and orientated towards family holidays, it offers a choice of mainly large pitches, some with lots of shade and some with less. It has a very pleasant ambience, a nice quiet pool area (with no noisy slides or toboggans) and it will undoubtedly appeal to families with younger children in particular. It is about five minutes' walk from the beach.

You might like to know

The sandy beach is just 300 m. away from the campsite, and the Mediterranean coast offers a choice of activities including sports and walking.

- ○ Beach on site
- ☑ Beach within 1 km
- ☑ Sandy beach
- ○ Blue Flag quality
- ○ Lifeguard *(high season)*
- ○ Sun lounger and/or deckchair hire
- ☑ Watersports *(e.g. sailing or windsurfing)*
- ☑ Snacks and drinks
- ☑ Sunshades/sunbeds
- ☑ Dogs allowed *(on the beach)*

Camping Club le Floride et l'Embouchure

Route de Saint Laurent, F-66423 Le Barcarès (Pyrénées-Orientales)
t: 04 68 86 11 75 e: campingfloride@aol.com
alanrogers.com/FR66290 www.floride.fr

Accommodation: ☑ Pitch ☑ Mobile home/chalet ○ Hotel/B&B ○ Apartment

Facilities: Four fully equipped toilet blocks on le Floride and two on l'Embouchure where 50 pitches near the beach have individual facilities. Facilities for babies and disabled visitors. Family shower room. Motorcaravan service point. Shop, bar, restaurant and takeaway (all 1/5-30/9). Excellent pool complex with indoor heated pool (all season). Excellent play area. Multisports court. Gym. Tennis. Multilingual entertainment and sports programmes (1/5-30/9). Bicycle hire. Charcoal barbecues are not permitted. Max. 1 dog. WiFi over site (charged). Off site: Beach 100 m. Fishing 1 km. Riding 1.5 km.

Open: 1 April - 30 September.

Directions: From A9 take exit 41 (Perpignan Nord) and follow signs for Canet and Le Barcarès via D83. At exit 9 follow D81 (Canet) then next left into Le Barcarès Village. Site is 1 km. on the left and right sides of the road.

GPS: 42.77855, 3.0301

Charges guide

Per unit incl. 2 persons and electricity	€ 15,00 - € 43,70
incl. individual sanitary facility	€ 19,00 - € 54,30
extra person	€ 2,90 - € 6,70
child (1-3 yrs)	no charge - € 3,90

A well established and multi-lingual, family run enterprise, le Floride et l'Embouchure is really two sites in one – l'Embouchure the smaller one with direct access to the beach and le Floride on the opposite side of the road. Fifty pitches have their own individual sanitary facility and in total the site offers 632 reasonably sized pitches, 280 for touring, all with 10A electricity. A good range of chalets and mobile homes are available for rent, including a recent Polynesian-style village. It is relatively inexpensive, especially outside the July and August peak period and the majority of the comprehensive facilities are open from 1st May. The busy town of Le Barcarès is within easy walking distance and has an increasing range of shops and supermarkets. The Voie Verte tarmac pathway runs for 15 km. from Le Barcarès to Rivesaltes alongside the River Agly, which borders l'Embouchure and is popular with cyclists, walkers, runners and roller skaters.

You might like to know

The site has direct access to the sea (100 m) and to a 3,000 m² aquatic complex with covered, heated swimming pool, paddling pool with games, a jacuzzi and fun slides.

☑ Beach on site
○ Beach within 1 km
☑ Sandy beach
☑ Blue Flag quality
☑ Lifeguard *(high season)*
☑ Sun lounger and/or deckchair hire
☑ Watersports *(e.g. sailing or windsurfing)*
☑ Snacks and drinks
☑ Sunshades/sunbeds
○ Dogs allowed *(on the beach)*

Facilities: Small supermarket, bar, restaurant with takeaway, outdoor swimming and paddling pools (all open July/Aug). Multisports court. Tennis. Minigolf. Boules. Playgrounds. Games room (1/05-14/09). Kids' club and programme of activities and entertainment (July/Aug). Communal barbecue. WiFi throughout (charged). Max. 1 dog per unit. Off site: Riding and fishing 1 km. Bicycle hire 2 km. Beach with watersports (boating, sailing, windsurfing, water skiing, diving, jet skis) 1.5 km. Perpignan 18 km. Spain 50 km.

Open: 11 April - 29 September.

Directions: Le Barcarès is 50 km. south of Narbonne and 18 km. northwest of Perpignan. From A9 leave at exit 41 (Perpignan Nord) follow signs for Le Barcarès, after 10 km, take exit 9 towards Canet, Toreilles, then first right to Le Barcarès village. Pass under the motorway and Les Tamaris is the second site on the left.

GPS: 42.77529, 3.020334

Charges guide

Per unit incl. 2 persons and electricity € 14,50 - € 34,00	
extra person € 5,00 - € 7,00	
child (4-6 yrs) no charge - € 5,00	
dog € 3,50	

France – Port Barcarès

Camping les Tamaris

Route de Saint Laurent, F-66420 Port Barcarès (Pyrénées-Orientales)
t: 04 68 86 08 18   e: camping-tamaris@orange.fr
alanrogers.com/FR66890 www.tamaris.com

Accommodation: ☑ Pitch ☑ Mobile home/chalet ○ Hotel/B&B ○ Apartment

Part of an extensive complex of campsites close to the pleasant village of Port Barcarès on the Mediterranean coast, and midway between Narbonne and the Spanish border, les Tamaris is largely dedicated to the 300 chalets and mobile homes (33 for hire), grouped in three concentric circles and in serried ranks. Sixteen touring pitches with electrical connections (10A Europlug) are available. The sandy beach is a 20 minute walk, as are the first of the shops, bars and restaurants of Le Barcarès. Regular markets are held here throughout the year and there is a busy port and marina. The Village des Pêcheurs pays tribute to the region's fishing heritage.

You might like to know

There is a choice of beaches within 7 km. with sun loungers, parasols, snacks and drinks. Don't miss Perpignan with its Castillet and Palais des Rois de Majorque.

- ○ Beach on site
- ☑ Beach within 1 km
- ☑ Sandy beach
- ○ Blue Flag quality
- ☑ Lifeguard *(high season)*
- ○ Sun lounger and/or deckchair hire
- ☑ Watersports *(e.g. sailing or windsurfing)*
- ☑ Snacks and drinks
- ☑ Sunshades/sunbeds
- ○ Dogs allowed *(on the beach)*

Facilities: Ten modern, well used but clean toilet blocks. Mostly Turkish WCs. Facilities for disabled visitors (but steep steps). Baby room. Washing machines. Fridge hire. Well stocked supermarket, bars, pizzeria (all open all season). No swimming pool. Excellent play area. Boats, pedaloes for hire. Wide range of watersports. Games, competitions (July/Aug). Children's club. Tennis. Multisports courts. Only gas and electric barbecues are allowed. Dogs are not accepted 10/7-21/8. WiFi throughout (charged). Off site: Bicycle hire 500 m. Riding and golf 15 km.

Open: 30 March - 31 October

Directions: From Bormes-les-Mimosas, head east on D559 to Le Lavandou. At roundabout, turn off D559 towards the sea on road signed Favière. After 2 km. turn left at site signs.

GPS: 43.11779, 6.35176

Charges guide

Per unit incl. 2 persons and electricity	€ 29,00 - € 45,00
extra person	€ 6,00 - € 10,00
child (under 7 yrs)	no charge - € 4,90
dog (not 10/7-21/8)	no charge

France – Bormes-les-Mimosas

Camp du Domaine

B.P. 207 La Favière, F-83230 Bormes-les-Mimosas (Var)
t: 04 94 71 03 12 e: mail@campdudomaine.com
alanrogers.com/FR83120 www.campdudomaine.com

Accommodation: ☑ Pitch ☑ Mobile home/chalet ○ Hotel/B&B ○ Apartment

Camp du Domaine, 3 km. south of Le Lavandou, is a large, attractive beach-side site with 1,200 pitches set in 45 hectares of pinewood, although surprisingly it does not give the impression of being so big. The pitches are large and most are reasonably level, 800 with 10A electricity. The most popular pitches are beside the beach, but the ones furthest away are generally larger and have more shade. Amongst the trees, many are more suitable for tents. The price for all the pitches is the same – smaller but near the beach or larger with shade. The beach is the attraction and everyone tries to get close. American motorhomes are not accepted. Despite its size, the site does not feel too busy, except perhaps around the supermarket. This is mainly because many pitches are hidden in the trees, the access roads are quite wide and it all covers quite a large area (some of the beach pitches are 600 m. from the entrance). Its popularity makes early reservation necessary over a long season (about mid June to mid Sept) as regular clients book from season to season.

You might like to know

On the beach you will find all manner of watersports, a sailing school, a diving school and beach volleyball (in high season). From Le Lavandou there are boat trips to the Iles d'Or (Port Cros and Porquerolles).

- ☑ Beach on site
- ○ Beach within 1 km
- ☑ Sandy beach
- ○ Blue Flag quality
- ☑ Lifeguard *(high season)*
- ☑ Sun lounger and/or deckchair hire
- ☑ Watersports *(e.g. sailing or windsurfing)*
- ☑ Snacks and drinks
- ☑ Sunshades/sunbeds
- ○ Dogs allowed *(on the beach)*

Facilities: Two clean sanitary blocks with controllable pushbutton showers. Wet room for disabled visitors. Laundry facilities. Play area. Boules. Mobile homes for rent. Dogs are not accepted 5/7-26/8. Children's club (4-12 yrs; July/Aug). New sports field. Off site: Le Lavandou 500 m. Nearest beach 800 m. Bicycle hire 800 m. Fishing 1.5 km. Sailing 2 km. Golf 10 km.

Open: 1 May - 5 October.

Directions: From Hyères (A570) head east on D98 to Bormes-les-Mimosas and then southeast on D559 to Le Lavandou. Then follow signs to the site.

GPS: 43.136047, 6.354416

Charges guide

Per unit incl. 2 persons and electricity € 18,00 - € 32,90
extra person € 4,30 - € 6,20
child (under 7 yrs) € 3,10 - € 4,40
dog (excl. 5/7-26/8) € 2,70 - € 3,90

France – Le Lavandou

Camping Saint Pons

Avenue Maréchal Juin, F-83190 Le Lavandou (Var)
t: 04 94 71 03 93 e: info@campingstpons.com
alanrogers.com/FR83680 www.campingstpons.com

Accommodation: ☑ Pitch ☑ Mobile home/chalet ○ Hotel/B&B ○ Apartment

Camping Saint Pons enjoys an attractive setting within walking distance of the delightful family resort of Le Lavandou. This is a relatively small, quiet and uncomplicated site extending over two hectares, with many flowering shrubs and bushes. There are 155 pitches here, well shaded and of a fair size. Most have electrical connections. A number of mobile homes are available for rent. There is no shop on site but there is a supermarket just 500 m. away. There is also a bar and restaurant next door. The Littoral cycle track runs close to the site and provides an appealing way of exploring the coast and a number of pretty Provençal villages. Saint Pons is a relaxed site with little by way of on-site entertainment which will be welcomed by many in this otherwise busy area. Le Lavandou is also one of the Riviera's more restrained resorts, named apparently after the river where local women came to do their washing because the water was so soft. The village boasts no fewer than 12 beaches, some wide and sandy, and others tiny, rocky coves. Good English is spoken.

You might like to know

There are no fewer than 12 beaches at Le Lavandou, including the Grande Plage, a fine sandy beach backed with palm trees.

- ○ Beach on site
- ☑ Beach within 1 km
- ☑ Sandy beach
- ☑ Blue Flag quality
- ☑ Lifeguard *(high season)*
- ☑ Sun lounger and/or deckchair hire
- ☑ Watersports *(e.g. sailing or windsurfing)*
- ☑ Snacks and drinks
- ☑ Sunshades/sunbeds
- ☑ Dogs allowed *(on the beach)*

Facilities: Three spacious sanitary blocks are clean and well maintained. Tennis court. Heated indoor pool, snacks and takeaway (all open all season). Max. 1 dog. WiFi throughout. Only gas barbecues permitted. Communal barbecue. Bicycle hire. Multisports ground. Off site: Beach 150 m. Bars, restaurant, and small shops nearby. Riding 2 km. Boat launching 11 km. Fishing 15 km. Golf 20 km.

Open: 12 April - 21 September.

Directions: From Longeville-sur-Mer follow signs for le Rocher towards La Tranche-sur-Mer. Turn right at first roundabout, following campsite signs to site on right.

GPS: 46.403767, -1.507183

Charges guide

Per unit incl. 2 persons
and electricity € 18,00 - € 32,00

extra person € 5,00 - € 9,00

child (0-5 yrs) no charge - € 6,00

dog € 5,00

France – Longeville-sur-Mer

Camping le Petit Rocher

1250 avenue de Docteur Mathevet, F-85560 Longeville-sur-Mer (Vendée)
t: 02 51 20 41 94   e: contact@camp-atlantique.com
alanrogers.com/FR85000   www.camp-atlantique.com

Accommodation: ☑ Pitch ☑ Mobile home/chalet ○ Hotel/B&B ○ Apartment

Le Petit Rocher has a seaside location (150 m. from the beach) set in a pine forest, with an air of peace and tranquillity. Although the area is undulating, the 132 good sized touring pitches are flat and arranged in terraces throughout the wooded area. Electricity hook-ups are available (10A Euro plugs) and there are adequate water points. A grassy play area for children is thoughtfully situated in a hollow, but has limited equipment. Various accommodation types are available to rent.

You might like to know

The site is close to Plage du Rocher, one of three safe family beaches in the area. They are backed by pine forests, which have cycle tracks and are ideal for hiking and horse riding.

○ Beach on site
☑ Beach within 1 km
☑ Sandy beach
☑ Blue Flag quality
☑ Lifeguard *(high season)*
○ Sun lounger and/or deckchair hire
☑ Watersports *(e.g. sailing or windsurfing)*
☑ Snacks and drinks
☑ Sunshades/sunbeds
☑ Dogs allowed *(on the beach)*

Facilities

Facilities: The main toilet block is very basic but clean, three others are open as needed. Controllable showers and washbasins in cubicles, facilities for babies and disabled visitors. Washing machines and dryers. Well stocked shop, bar and restaurant, snack bars and takeaway (all season). New water park for 2014 with indoor and outdoor swimming pools. Fitness room. Hammam, sauna, massage and hairdressing for 2014. Adventure playground. Bouncy castle. Tennis. Basketball. Beach volleyball. Minigolf. Small fenced fishing lake. Bicycle hire. Activity programme (all season). Children's clubs and entertainment at busy times. WiFi over site (charged). Only gas barbecues allowed. Accommodation for rent. Off site: Shops, restaurants and bars in Olonne-sur-Mer 1.5 km. Golf 2 km. Riding and Les Sables 5 km. Beaches (shuttle bus in high season), boat launching, sailing and watersports.

Open: 13 April - 29 September.

Directions: Olonne-sur-Mer is 5 km north of Les Sables d'Olonne. From A87 at La Roche-sur-Yon, head southwest on D160 towards Les Sables d'Olonne and leave at exit for Olonne-sur-Mer (D80). Continue on this road, crossing D760 and you will see the site (well signed) on right. Arrivals must use loop in car park opposite while booking in.

GPS: 46.53172, -1.758279

Charges guide

Per unit incl. 2 persons and electricity	€ 22,00 - € 40,00
extra person	€ 5,00 - € 9,00
child (0-4 yrs)	no charge - € 6,00

France – Olonne-sur-Mer

MS Vacances Camping Le Trianon

95 rue du Maréchal Joffre, F-85340 Olonne-sur-Mer (Vendée)
t: 02 53 81 70 00 e: reservation@ms-vacances.com
alanrogers.com/FR85005 www.ms-vacances.com

Accommodation: ☑ Pitch ☑ Mobile home/chalet ○ Hotel/B&B ○ Apartment

On the edge of the bustling village of Olonne-sur-Mer, close to the popular resort of Les Sables d'Olonne, le Trianon is a large site very much geared to mobile homes and chalets, half of which (220) are available for rent. There are 100 touring pitches scattered amongst the statics. They vary in size and shape but all have water taps and drainage, with electricity (10A) nearby; there is plenty of shade. The site is under new ownership and there are ambitious development plans. Nearby Olonne-sur-Mer has shops, bars, restaurants and a large supermarket. Fashionable Les Sables is justly famous for its many excellent seafood restaurants, and maintains an important fishing fleet; it also has a good zoo and a wide range of amenities and services. The nearest beach is about 5 km. away, but there are many others to choose from, including Les Sables' famous Grande Plage. Reception has information on the area's impressive range of attractions, which include adventure parks, gardens, museums, theme parks and unusual activities such as Vélorail.

You might like to know

This peaceful, shady site offers plenty of opportunities for relaxing and for enjoying the many activities available. A shuttle bus to the beach is available.

- ○ Beach on site
- ○ Beach within 1 km
- ☑ Sandy beach
- ☑ Blue Flag quality
- ☑ Lifeguard (high season)
- ☑ Sun lounger and/or deckchair hire
- ☑ Watersports (e.g. sailing or windsurfing)
- ☑ Snacks and drinks
- ☑ Sunshades/sunbeds
- ☑ Dogs allowed (on the beach)

MS Vacances Camping Club Les Brunelles

Le Bouil, F-85560 Longeville-sur-Mer (Vendée)
t: 02 53 81 70 00 e: reservation@ms-vacances.com
alanrogers.com/FR85440 www.ms-vacances.com

Accommodation: ☑ Pitch ☑ Mobile home/chalet ○ Hotel/B&B ○ Apartment

Facilities: Four well maintained and modernised toilet blocks have British and Turkish style toilets and washbasins, both open style and in cabins. Laundry facilities. Shop, restaurant, takeaway and large modern, airy bar (all season). Covered pool with jacuzzi (all season). Outdoor heated pool with slides and paddling pools (12/5-27/9). Tennis. Bicycle hire. Max. 1 dog. WiFi over site (charged). Gas barbecues only. Off site: Riding 3 km. Good, supervised, sandy beach 900 m. St Vincent-sur-Jard 2 km. Golf 20 km.

Open: 12 April - 27 September.

Directions: Longeville-sur-Mer is 28 km. south from the A87 exit 32 at La Roche-sur-Yon via the D747 (La Tranche), D949 (Les Sables) and in 3 km, D91. Site is 3.5 km. southwest of the village and is signed from the D21 (Jard-sur-Mer).

GPS: 46.41330, -1.52313

Charges guide

Per unit incl. 2 persons and electricity	€ 22,00 - € 40,00
incl. water and waste water	€ 26,00 - € 45,00
extra person	€ 5,00 - € 9,00
child (under 5 yrs)	no charge - € 6,00
dog	€ 5,00

This is a well managed site with a wide range of facilities and a varied programme of high season entertainment for all the family. A busy site in high season, there are plenty of activities to keep children happy and occupied. In 2007, les Brunelles was combined with an adjacent campsite to provide 612 pitches of which 142 are for touring units; all have electricity (10A) and 20 of the new touring pitches also have water and a drain. All are 100 sq.m. to allow easier access for larger units. On the original les Brunelles site, the touring pitches are all level on sandy grass and separated by hedges, away from most of the mobile homes. A large aquapark provides a swimming pool of 1,000 sq.m. with indoor and outdoor pools, slides, a sauna, steam room, jacuzzi, and a fitness centre. A good, supervised, sandy beach is 900 m. away.

You might like to know

There are three sandy beaches within easy reach, as well as surfing and sailing schools. In July and August, the little train at Longeville runs to the market, the beach and the shops.

- ☑ Beach on site
- ☑ Beach within 1 km
- ☑ Sandy beach
- ○ Blue Flag quality
- ○ Lifeguard *(high season)*
- ☑ Sun lounger and/or deckchair hire
- ☑ Watersports *(e.g. sailing or windsurfing)*
- ☑ Snacks and drinks
- ☑ Sunshades/sunbeds
- ☑ Dogs allowed *(on the beach)*

Perran Sands Holiday Park

Perranporth TR6 0AQ (Cornwall)
t: 01872 573551   e: nick.cook@bourne-leisure.co.uk
alanrogers.com/UK0135   www.haventouring.com

Accommodation: ☑ Pitch ☑ Mobile home/chalet ○ Hotel/B&B ○ Apartment

Facilities: Three basic toilet blocks (no electrical points) with two family rooms with facilities for babies and campers with disabilities. Launderette. Supermarket with bakery and off licence. Gift shop. Café/bar and grill with terrace. Fish and chips, Burger King, Papa John's takeaway pizza. Sports bar. Heated indoor fun pool with flume and heated outdoor pool (28/5-3/9). Multisports court. Mini 10-pin bowling. Amusement arcade. Pool tables. Surf school (equipment hire). Two family show/entertainment bars (one open outside July/Aug). Kids' club for all ages. Soft play area. Playland. Road train. Accommodation to hire. WiFi. Bus service. Off site: Fishing 2 miles. Newquay 8 miles. Eden Project 24 miles.

Open: 1 April - 31 October.

Directions: From Goonhaven take road for Perranporth. Site entrance on right before going down the hill.
GPS: 50.359357, -5.143635

Charges guide

Per unit incl. 2 persons and electricity	£ 8,00 - £ 61,00
extra person no charge	- £ 2,00
dog	£ 3,00

An amazing site on grassy sand dunes with over 1,100 pitches in total (350 for touring units), with numerous mobile homes dotted amongst the dunes. The dedicated touring area has its own wardens and a separate reception in high season. It is a village in its own right, with all the facilities that you could need – shops, restaurants, bars, entertainment. The entertainment centre is the heart of the site and is a short walk from the camping area. Pitches are on sandy grass, marked by fencing, some level, some sloping, many with rabbit holes, 280 have 10A electricity and a few hardstandings. It is possible to hire tents or even yurts. To get around the site, you will need the Perran Puffer road train. A magnificent sandy beach is just over the next dune, popular with surfers, but for something a little more relaxing there are indoor and outdoor heated pools on site, both with lifeguards. If you take advantage of everything on offer you won't need to leave the site, but the surfing paradise of Newquay is probably worth a visit and the Eden Project is not to be missed.

You might like to know

Perran Sands is a top surfing beach and the holiday park offers on-site surfing lessons and equipment hire.

○ Beach on site
☑ Beach within 1 km
☑ Sandy beach
○ Blue Flag quality
☑ Lifeguard *(high season)*
○ Sun lounger and/or deckchair hire
☑ Watersports *(e.g. sailing or windsurfing)*
☑ Snacks and drinks
○ Sunshades/sunbeds
☑ Dogs allowed *(on the beach)*

Facilities: Five modern toilet blocks provide showers, two family bathrooms, baby bath, laundry facilities and provision for disabled visitors. Well stocked supermarket with bread made on site (from late May). Hire shop. Bars (with TV), restaurant, café and takeaway. Entertainment (every night in season). Pool complex with heated outdoor pool, paddling pool, sunbathing decks, solarium, sauna and massage chair. Health and beauty salon. Super Fort Knox style adventure playground, crazy golf, Kiddies Club. Amusement arcade and bowling alley. Teenagers' room. 18-hole pitch and putt with golf pro shop. Bicycle hire. Coarse fishing with three lakes. Dogs are accepted in two fields only. Only limited facilities open at Easter and from 8 Sept. Off site: Riding within 2 miles. Bicycle hire and boat launching 4 miles.

Open: 23 May - 14 September.

Directions: From A3075 approach to Newquay-Perranporth road, turn towards Cubert and Holywell Bay. Continue through Cubert to park on the right.
GPS: 50.384983, -5.128933

Charges guide

Per unit incl. 2 persons and electricity £ 27,55 - £ 46,45	
extra person £ 5,85 - £ 10,95	
child (3-14 yrs) £ 1,60 - £ 7,95	
dog £ 4,40 - £ 5,60	

Families and couples only. Many special discounts.

United Kingdom – Newquay

Trevornick Holiday Park

Holywell Bay, Newquay TR8 5PW (Cornwall)
t: 01637 830531 e: bookings@trevornick.co.uk
alanrogers.com/UK0220 www.trevornick.co.uk

Accommodation: ☑ Pitch ○ Mobile home/chalet ○ Hotel/B&B ○ Apartment

Trevornick, once a working farm, is a modern, busy and well run family touring park providing a very wide range of amenities, close to one of Cornwall's finest beaches. A modern reception with welcoming staff sets the tone for your holiday. The park is well managed with facilities and standards constantly monitored. It has grown to provide caravanners and campers (no holiday caravans but 56 very well equipped Eurotents) with some 550 large grass pitches (350 with 10A electricity and 55 fully serviced with electricity, water, drainage and TV connection with DVD channel) on five level fields and two terraced areas. There are few trees but some good views. With 'all singing, all dancing' facilities for fun packed family holidays, the farm buildings now provide the setting for the Farm Club. Recently refurbished, it provides much entertainment, from bingo and quizzes to shows, discos and cabaret. The Stables Grill also opens for breakfast and the Hungry Horse provides takeaway food.

You might like to know

Surfing is one of the most popular sports in Cornwall and Trevornick Holiday Park is only a short walk away from the beautiful Holywell Bay beach, which attracts surfers from far and wide.

○ Beach on site
☑ Beach within 1 km
☑ Sandy beach
○ Blue Flag quality
○ Lifeguard *(high season)*
○ Sun lounger and/or deckchair hire
☑ Watersports *(e.g. sailing or windsurfing)*
○ Snacks and drinks
○ Sunshades/sunbeds
○ Dogs allowed *(on the beach)*

Facilities: Four basic toilet blocks with good hot water are spread amongst the terraces. The newer shower block has separate toilets opposite. Shop. Self-service food bar providing good value meals and breakfast (main season and B.Hs). Two bars and full entertainment programme. Heated indoor and outdoor pools both with paddling pool areas. Fenced play area on bark with plenty of equipment. Ball area with nets. Crazy golf. Kingpin bowling. Off site: Beach 15 minutes walk or 0.5 miles. Riding next door. Golf, bicycle hire and freshwater fishing 0.5 miles.

Open: 1 April - 30 October.

Directions: Follow A361 from Barnstaple through Braunton towards Ilfracombe. At Mullacott Cross roundabout turn left for Woolacombe (B3343). Site clearly signed on left as you go down the hill into the village.

GPS: 51.17145, -4.191833

Charges guide

Per person (incl. electricity)	£ 5,00 - £ 15,00
child (4-15 yrs)	£ 2,50 - £ 7,50
dog	£ 5,00

Woolacombe Sands Holiday Park

Beach Road, Woolacombe EX34 7AF (Devon)
t: 01271 870569 e: lifesabeach@woolacombe-sands.co.uk
alanrogers.com/UK0735 www.woolacombe.co.uk

Accommodation: ☑ Pitch ☑ Mobile home/chalet ○ Hotel/B&B ○ Apartment

With sea views and within walking distance of Woolacombe's lovely sandy beach, this family park has been terraced out of the valley side as you drop down into the village. Apart from its smart entrance, it has been left natural. The pond and stream at the bottom are almost hidden with gated access to the National Trust fields across the valley. The 200 terraced, level grass pitches, all with 16A electricity, are accessed by gravel roads with some good up-and-down walking needed to the toilet blocks (may pose a problem for visitors with disabilities). Some 50 mobile homes and 14 bungalows are in the more central area, and tents tend to be placed on the bottom terraces. The park boasts both indoor and outdoor pools (accessed by code) with a full time attendant. Upstairs from the indoor pool is a very pleasant conservatory seating area with great views and an outside seating area adjacent to it. A good plus factor is the fact that all facilities open when the site opens.

You might like to know

Situated on the North Devon coast two miles west of Bideford, the BIG Sheep (a key member of Devon's Top Attractions) is an all-weather family attraction devoted to sheep and offering a wide range of indoor and outdoor activities.

○ Beach on site
☑ Beach within 1 km
☑ Sandy beach
☑ Blue Flag quality
☑ Lifeguard *(high season)*
○ Sun lounger and/or deckchair hire
☑ Watersports *(e.g. sailing or windsurfing)*
☑ Snacks and drinks
○ Sunshades/sunbeds
☑ Dogs allowed *(on the beach)*

Facilities

Facilities: Good toilet blocks adjacent to the pitches, well maintained and heated, include roomy showers, some with washbasins en-suite. Baths on payment. Unit for disabled visitors. Facilities for babies. Laundry. Gas supplies. Motorcaravan service point. Large general shop (25/3-2/11). Restaurant, bars and takeaway (all 25/3-14/4, 3/5-15/9, 27/9-3/10, and 26/10-1/11). Heated swimming pools, outdoor 3/5-1/9, indoor all year. Fitness centre. Tennis. Crazy golf. Playground. Nature trail. Amusement centre with pool, table tennis and amusement machines. Children's room. Soft play area. WiFi over site (charged). Dogs are not accepted. Off site: Regular minibus service to Paignton (timetable at reception) and public services from outside the park. Fishing, bicycle hire, riding and golf all within 2 miles.

Open: All year.

Directions: Park is south of Paignton in Goodrington Road between A379 coast road and B3203 ring road and is well signed on both.

GPS: 50.413533, -3.568667

Charges guide

Per unit incl. 2 persons and electricity	£ 17,20 - £ 38,40
tent pitch incl. 2 persons	£ 14,00 - £ 34,10
extra person	£ 4,90
child (4-14 yrs)	£ 3,70

Max. 6 persons per reservation.

United Kingdom – Paignton

Beverley Park

Goodrington Road, Paignton TQ4 7JE (Devon)
t: 01803 661978 e: info@beverley-holidays.co.uk
alanrogers.com/UK0870 www.beverley-holidays.co.uk

Accommodation: ☑ Pitch ☑ Mobile home/chalet ○ Hotel/B&B ○ Apartment

Beverley Park is an amazing holiday centre catering for every need. It has been developed and run by the Jeavons family for over 50 years to very high standards. It is popular, busy and attractively landscaped with marvellous views over Torbay. The pools, a cabaret area, bars and entertainment, are all run in an efficient and orderly manner. The park has 184 caravan holiday homes and 23 lodges, mainly around the central complex. There are 165 touring pitches in the lower areas of the park, all reasonably sheltered, some with views across the bay and some on slightly sloping ground. All pitches can take awnings and have 16A electricity (15 m. cable), 42 have hardstanding and are fully serviced. Tents are accepted and a limited number of tent pitches have electrical connections. The park is open all year and reservations are essential for caravans in high season. Entertainment is organised at Easter and from early May in the Starlight Cabaret bar. There are indoor and outdoor pools, each one heated and supervised. A member of the Best of British group.

You might like to know

No visit to Devon would be complete without a day at Dartmoor's famous Becky Falls, where there really is something for everyone to enjoy. Set within a spectacular ancient valley, the Falls have been attracting visitors for over 100 years.

○ Beach on site
☑ Beach within 1 km
☑ Sandy beach
☑ Blue Flag quality
○ Lifeguard *(high season)*
○ Sun lounger and/or deckchair hire
☑ Watersports *(e.g. sailing or windsurfing)*
○ Snacks and drinks
○ Sunshades/sunbeds
○ Dogs allowed *(on the beach)*

Facilities: Two modern toilet blocks with all necessary facilities including two family rooms with bath, showers, basin and WC, and four rooms with shower, basin and WC. Washing machine and dryer. Well stocked shop (19/3-31/10). Good, large adventure playground and plenty of space for ball games. Crazy golf. Giant chess and golf course adjacent to the site. Bicycle hire. WiFi throughout (charged). Off site: Beach 0.5 miles. Fishing and shop 1 mile. Golf and riding 2 miles. Bird Reserve at Cley. National Trust properties. North Norfolk Tourist Railway. Boat trips.

Open: 19 March - 31 October.

Directions: Site is beside the A149 coast road between East and West Runton.

GPS: 52.93742, 1.26250

Charges guide

Per unit incl. 2 persons and electricity	£ 16,10 - £ 20,15
extra person	£ 2,60 - £ 2,85
child (4-16 yrs)	£ 1,05 - £ 1,20
dog	£ 2,15 - £ 3,80

United Kingdom – Cromer

Woodhill Park

Cromer Road, East Runton, Cromer NR27 9PX (Norfolk)
t: 01263 512242 e: info@woodhill-park.com
alanrogers.com/UK3500 www.woodhill-park.com

Accommodation: ☑ Pitch ☑ Mobile home/chalet ○ Hotel/B&B ○ Apartment

Woodhill is a seaside site with good views and a traditional atmosphere. It is situated on the clifftop, in a large, gently sloping, open grassy field, with 300 marked touring pitches. Of these, 210 have 16A electricity, seven are fully serviced and many have wonderful views over the surrounding coastline and countryside. A small number of holiday homes are available with magnificent sea views. Although the site is fenced, there is access to the clifftop path which takes you to the beach. Locally, it is possible to take a boat trip to see the seals off Blakeney Point. Nearby attractions include the Shire Horse Centre at West Runton and the North Norfolk Steam Railway. Green technology plays a major role with solar panels added to one of the block roofs to heat the water. Access to nearby towns and resorts is available using the local bus stop outside the entrance, or by the tourist railway.

You might like to know

The site overlooks a long sandy beach with rock pools - ideal for crabbing. There are several coastal walks to enjoy and nearby trips to see the seals at Blakeney Point.

○ Beach on site
☑ Beach within 1 km
☑ Sandy beach
☑ Blue Flag quality
☑ Lifeguard *(high season)*
○ Sun lounger and/or deckchair hire
☑ Watersports *(e.g. sailing or windsurfing)*
☑ Snacks and drinks
○ Sunshades/sunbeds
☑ Dogs allowed *(on the beach)*

Skipsea Sands Holiday Park

Mill Lane, Skipsea YO25 8TZ (East Yorkshire)
t: 0871 664 9812   e: skipsea.sands@park-resorts.com
alanrogers.com/UK4496   www.park-resortstouring.com/skipseasands

Accommodation: ☑ Pitch ☑ Mobile home/chalet ○ Hotel/B&B ○ Apartment

This well established holiday park is now owned by Park Resorts and is primarily dedicated to caravan holiday homes, of which there are 625 privately owned and 70 to rent.
There is however a pleasantly laid out touring park occupying its own corner of the site and bordered by an attractive duck pond and a large playing area (both well fenced). The 91 marked, level pitches (some occupied by seasonal caravans) are separated by hedges and all have 16A electricity; some also have water, drainage and sewerage connections. The leisure facilities are outstanding and a full daily programme of activities and entertainment is offered for children and adults. Situated on the cliffs on the Yorkshire coast, south of Bridlington, beaches are either a good walk or a short drive away. There is a wide choice of possible days out: Beverley or York, each with its Minster and its horse racing; Spurn Point or Bempton Cliffs (RSPB); Cruckley Animal Farm or Bondville Miniature Village; Bridlington's beaches and its Harbour Heritage Museum.

You might like to know

There is a good choice of beaches within easy reach of the campsite, including the popular family resorts of Bridlington and Scarborough.

○ Beach on site
☑ Beach within 1 km
☑ Sandy beach
○ Blue Flag quality
○ Lifeguard (high season)
○ Sun lounger and/or deckchair hire
○ Watersports (e.g. sailing or windsurfing)
○ Snacks and drinks
○ Sunshades/sunbeds
☑ Dogs allowed (on the beach)

Facilities: Two heated toilet blocks have been refurbished, with pushbutton showers, open washbasins and en-suite facilities for disabled visitors. Basic chemical disposal and motorcaravan service point. Washing machines and dryers. Well stocked shop. Bar, coffee shop and restaurant with takeaway. Leisure centre with sports hall, 10-pin bowling, heated indoor swimming pool, jacuzzi, sauna and steam room. Fitness centre with gym and sunbed. Games Kingdom with electronic games and Kids' Zone. Fishing in duck pond (charged). WiFi (charged). Off site: Buses from park gates. Village with shops, pub, restaurant 1 mile. Beach 0.25 mile (on foot) or 4 miles (by car). Golf 3 miles. Boat launching 6 miles. Riding and sailing 9 miles.

Open: 1 March - 31 October.

Directions: Skipsea is 20 miles northeast of Hull and 10 miles south of Bridlington. From Humber Bridge or from M62, take A63 to Hull, east of city follow signs to join A165 towards Bridlington. After 18 miles, turn east on B1249 to Skipsea. In village, turn right then left to site (signed).
GPS: 53.98957, -0.20716

Charges guide

Per unit incl. all services	£ 11,00 - £ 46,00
tent pitch	£ 7,00 - £ 39,00
dog	£ 1,00 - £ 3,00

Facilities: The toilet block is of an excellent standard including washbasins in cubicles, facilities for disabled visitors and a baby room. Fully equipped laundry room. Dishwashing room and further sinks under cover. Motorcaravan service point. Gas available. Local tradesmen visit each morning selling milk, bread and newspapers. New play area. Riding. Dry ski slope. Toboggan ride. Late arrivals area (with electricity). Off site: Amenities of the country park. Shops 1 and 2.5 miles. Beach 1 mile (dogs are restricted on the beach May-Sept). Jack Nicklaus-designed golf course 4 miles.

Open: 23 March - 7 January.

Directions: Leave M4 at exit 48 onto A4138 (Llanelli). After 4 miles turn right onto A484 at roundabout (Carmarthen). Continue for 7 miles to Pembrey. Follow brown country park signs in preference to sat nav. The country park is signed off the A484 in Pembrey village; site entrance is on right 100 yds. before park gates.

GPS: 51.6823, -4.2979

Charges guide

Per person £ 5,90 - £ 8,00	
child (5-17 yrs) £ 1,60 - £ 3,10	
pitch incl. electricity (non-member) £ 16,20 - £ 19,90	

Pembrey Country Park Caravan Club Site

Pembrey, Llanelli SA16 0EJ (Carmarthenshire)
t: 01554 834369
alanrogers.com/UK5940 www.caravanclub.co.uk

Accommodation: ☑ Pitch ☑ Mobile home/chalet ○ Hotel/B&B ○ Apartment

Set on the edge of a 520-acre country park, this popular Caravan Club site enjoys a wonderful location with a vast range of outdoor activities, including the use of a seven-mile stretch of safe, sandy beach a mile away. Well sheltered, the site is set in 12-acre grounds and provides 130 touring pitches, of which 68 are on hardstanding for caravans and motorcaravans. All are equipped with 16A electricity. Thoughtful landscaping has included the planting of many species of trees and a circular, one-way tarmac road provides easy access. Sensibly placed service points provide fresh water and waste disposal of all types. RAF jets do practise in this area (although becoming less frequent and generally not flying at the weekend). There may be occasional noise from the nearby motor racing circuit. However, the real plus for this site is its proximity to the Country Park – access to this is free on foot or bicycle direct from the site, or reception can organise a special weekly car pass for around £12. The nearest section of beach is a 20 minute walk.

You might like to know

Cefn Sidan beach, an 8-mile stretch of golden sand described as one of Europe's best beaches, is approximately one mile from the campsite.

- ○ Beach on site
- ○ Beach within 1 km
- ☑ Sandy beach
- ☑ Blue Flag quality
- ☑ Lifeguard *(high season)*
- ○ Sun lounger and/or deckchair hire
- ○ Watersports *(e.g. sailing or windsurfing)*
- ○ Snacks and drinks
- ○ Sunshades/sunbeds
- ○ Dogs allowed *(on the beach)*

Facilities: Two traditional toilet blocks offer adequate facilities for the whole family, including those for disabled campers (a long way from some pitches). Motorcaravan service point. Small shop (Easter-1/11). Play area. WiFi (charged). Off site: Beach 200 yds. Fishing 300 yds. Boat launching 1 mile. Riding 5 miles. Golf 9 miles.

Open: 1 March - 8 January.

Directions: Park is off the A496 road north of Barmouth. Entrance is on left down a steep drive.

GPS: 52.73300, -4.06618

Charges guide

Per unit incl. 2 persons and electricity	£ 18,00 - £ 31,00
extra person	£ 4,00
child (2-14 yrs)	£ 2,00
first dog free, extra dog	£ 1,00

Plus £2 per night for certain weekends. Mid-season and Christmas/New Year offers.

United Kingdom – Barmouth

Hendre Mynach Touring Park

Llanaber Road, Barmouth LL42 1YR (Gwynedd)
t: 01341 280262 e: mynach@lineone.net
alanrogers.com/UK6370 www.hendremynach.co.uk

Accommodation: ☑ Pitch ☑ Mobile home/chalet ○ Hotel/B&B ○ Apartment

A large family park, stretching out along the beach on the outskirts of Barmouth. Colourful flowers brighten the steep entrance to this site (help is available to get out if you are worried). Of the 240 pitches, all for touring, 60 are on hardstanding with 10A electricity, and 39 are fully serviced. The beach is only 200 yards away but is separated from the park by a railway line. It can be crossed by pedestrian operated gates, which could be a worry for those with young children. The quaint old seaside and fishing town of Barmouth is about a 30 minute walk along the prom. Here you will find 'everything'. Reception will provide leaflets with maps of local walks. Snowdonia National Park and mountain railway, the famous Ffestiniog railway, and castles and lakes everywhere provide plenty to see and do.

You might like to know

Aberdovey was once an important shipbuilding town, but is now a popular resort on the River Dyfi with a fine Blue Flag beach.

- ○ Beach on site
- ☑ Beach within 1 km
- ☑ Sandy beach
- ☑ Blue Flag quality
- ○ Lifeguard *(high season)*
- ○ Sun lounger and/or deckchair hire
- ☑ Watersports *(e.g. sailing or windsurfing)*
- ○ Snacks and drinks
- ○ Sunshades/sunbeds
- ○ Dogs allowed *(on the beach)*

Facilities: The single Portacabin style toilet block is clean, heated and adequate. No specific facilities for disabled visitors or babies. Laundry facilities. Games room. Direct beach access. Sea swimming and fishing. Canoeing. WiFi (in the games room; charged). Accommodation to rent. Off site: Well stocked village shop 100 yds. Kintyre Way walking trail. Whisky distilleries. Golf.

Open: April - mid October.

Directions: Approaching from Glasgow (Erskine Bridge), take the A82 towards Crianlarich, past Loch Lomond. At Tarbet take the A83 towards Campbeltown, through Inveraray, Lochgilphead and Tarbert (Loch Fyne) and on to Muasdale Village, from where the site is well signed.

GPS: 55.597307, -5.686058

Charges guide

Per unit incl. 2 persons and electricity	£ 17,50 - £ 19,50
extra person	£ 2,00
child (5-15 yrs)	£ 1,25
dog	£ 1,25

United Kingdom – Tarbert

Muasdale Holiday Park

Muasdale, Tarbert PA29 6XD (Argyll and Bute)
t: 01583 421207 e: enquiries@muasdaleholidays.com
alanrogers.com/UK7250 www.muasdaleholidays.com

Accommodation: ☑ Pitch ☑ Mobile home/chalet ○ Hotel/B&B ○ Apartment

Muasdale Holiday Park has a beach-side location with fine views of the sea and islands, between Campbeltown and Tarbert on Kintyre's west coast. This is a small, friendly site of just 16 pitches with ten for touring units, five for tents and one used for a caravan holiday home to rent. The pitches are situated on a level, grass field, all with unobstructed sea views. All have electrical connections. You are advised to anchor tents and awnings securely as the winds are sometimes strong and gusty. The beach is a magnificent expanse of white sand with rock pools and an abundance of wildlife. The sunsets are frequently breathtaking. Sea canoeing and sea fishing are both popular. The site prides itself on its 'get away from it all' nature. There are very few amenities here but there is a well stocked village shop just 100 m. away. There is no bar or restaurant. Barbecues are permitted on site, and campfires are also possible on the beach, provided that proper care is taken.

You might like to know

There are many rock pools to explore, and sea fishing and sea canoeing are popular.

- ☑ Beach on site
- ○ Beach within 1 km
- ☑ Sandy beach
- ○ Blue Flag quality
- ○ Lifeguard *(high season)*
- ○ Sun lounger and/or deckchair hire
- ☑ Watersports *(e.g. sailing or windsurfing)*
- ○ Snacks and drinks
- ○ Sunshades/sunbeds
- ○ Dogs allowed *(on the beach)*

Facilities: The toilet facilities can be heated. Showers have no divider or seat. Laundry. Motorcaravan service point. The Anchorage restaurant at the entrance to the park (used as reception at quiet times) serves meals at reasonable prices, cooked to order (I/4-30/9). Boat launching. Fishing permits can be arranged. Off site: Village with shop and post office, gas is available from the petrol station and mobile banks visit regularly.

Open: Easter/1 April - 30 September, but phone first to check.

Directions: Park is by Scourie village on A894 road in northwest Sutherland.

GPS: 58.351417, -5.156767

Charges guide

Per unit incl. 2 persons electricity
£ 24,40 - £ 29,40

No credit cards.

United Kingdom – Scourie

Scourie Caravan & Camping Park

Harbour Road, Scourie IV27 4TG (Highland)
t: 01971 502060
alanrogers.com/UK7730

Accommodation: ☑ Pitch ☑ Mobile home/chalet ○ Hotel/B&B ○ Apartment

Mr Mackenzie's family now run this park. There are a number of firm terraces with 60 pitches which gives it an attractive layout – there is nothing regimented here. Perched on the edge of the bay in an elevated position, practically everyone has a view of the sea and a short walk along the shore footpath leads to a small sandy beach. The park has tarmac and gravel access roads, with well drained grass and hardstanding pitches, some with 10A electric hook-ups. A few are on an area which is unfenced from the rocks (young children would need to be supervised here). Reception, alongside the modern toilet block, contains a wealth of tourist information and maps. There are very good facilities for disabled visitors on the park and at the restaurant, although the ramps leading to them are a little steep. Mr Mackenzie claims that this is the only caravan park in the world from where, depending on the season, you can see palm trees, Highland cattle and Great Northern divers from your pitch. Red throated divers have also been seen.

You might like to know

The small sandy beach is a short walk from the site. It has crystal clear water and is great for swimming and fishing from the rocks. There is also a bird hide.

○ Beach on site
☑ Beach within 1 km
☑ Sandy beach
○ Blue Flag quality
○ Lifeguard *(high season)*
○ Sun lounger and/or deckchair hire
○ Watersports *(e.g. sailing or windsurfing)*
○ Snacks and drinks
○ Sunshades/sunbeds
○ Dogs allowed *(on the beach)*

Strandhill Caravan & Camping Park

Strandhill (Co. Sligo)
t: 071 916 8111   e: strandhillcvp@eircom.net
alanrogers.com/IR8695   www.sligocaravanandcamping.ie

Accommodation: ☑ Pitch ◯ Mobile home/chalet ◯ Hotel/B&B ◯ Apartment

This seaside park is located on 20 acres of undulating grass on a sandy base, with natural protection from the onshore breezes of the famous Strandhill beach. There are 55 hardstanding pitches for caravans and motorcaravans, with electricity and ample water points, and two camping areas for tents, one with views of the sea and the second more sheltered. Throughout the site many hollows provide ideal pitches for tents. Strandhill, world recognised as a surfing Mecca, also provides activities for all the family. There are miles of sandy beach and dunes, and the Knocknarea Mountain is a popular choice for walkers. The Megalithic Tombs at Carrowmore, older than the Pyramids at Giza, are 5 km. away and the flat beach at Culleenmore is 2 km. Strandhill provides an excellent touring base for the Benbulban, Yeats' Country and Lough Gill's Isle of Inisfree combining nature, heritage, and fable. There are two flights daily into nearby Sligo airport.

You might like to know

Swimming is not advised at this beach due to strong tides and currents.

- ☑ Beach on site
- ◯ Beach within 1 km
- ☑ Sandy beach
- ◯ Blue Flag quality
- ◯ Lifeguard *(high season)*
- ◯ Sun lounger and/or deckchair hire
- ☑ Watersports *(e.g. sailing or windsurfing)*
- ☑ Snacks and drinks
- ◯ Sunshades/sunbeds
- ◯ Dogs allowed *(on the beach)*

Facilities: The toilet block (keys provided on deposit) is clean and fresh with hot showers (token €1.50), electric hand dryers and hairdryer. New reception building, including TV room, games room, campers' kitchen, laundry and a well equipped facility for disabled visitors. WiFi over part of site (charged). Automatic gate and door control. Off site: Children's playground adjacent. Public transport from village. Shops, restaurants, takeaway, pubs and ATM are just beyond the park's boundary in the village. Strandhill golf course 500 m. Bicycle hire within 1 km. Riding 2 km. Swimming pool and sports centre in Sligo 8 km.

Open: Easter - 30 September.

Directions: Strandhill is 8 km. west of Sligo city on the R292. Site is on the airport road.

GPS: 54.27242, -8.60448

Charges guide

Per unit incl. 2 persons	€ 20,00
plus 2 children	€ 22,00
electricity (10A)	€ 4,00
extra person	€ 3,00 - € 5,00

Facilities: Two modern toilet blocks serve the site, one at the entrance gate beside reception and the other in a central position. Heated facilities include WCs, washbasins and hot showers (on payment). Hairdryers. Laundry with irons and ironing boards. En-suite facilities for disabled visitors at reception block. Play area. TV/games room. Watersports enthusiasts can enjoy surfing, kite surfing, canoeing and board sailing on Keel Strand and Lough. Fishing trips can be arranged. WiFi throughout (charged). Off site: Bicycle hire and golf 200 m. Riding 6 km. In the village there is a food shop, takeaway, restaurants and music at night in the pubs.

Open: Easter - mid September.

Directions: From Achill Sound follow the R319 for 13 km. Site is on the left before Keel village.

GPS: 53.97535, -10.0779

Charges guide

Per unit incl. 2 persons
and electricity € 18,00 - € 21,00

child € 2,00

extra person € 3,00

Keel Sandybanks Touring Park

Keel, Achill Island (Co. Mayo)
t: 098 432 11   e: info@achillcamping.com
alanrogers.com/IR8730   www.achillcamping.com

Accommodation: ☑ Pitch ☑ Mobile home/chalet ○ Hotel/B&B ○ Apartment

This is a park offering a taste of island life and the opportunity to relax in dramatic, scenic surroundings. Achill, Ireland's largest island, is 24 km. long and 19 km. wide and is connected to the mainland by a bridge. The wide open site is situated beside the Blue Flag beach near Keel village. Although there are static holiday mobile homes on this site, the 84 touring pitches are kept separate. There are 50 pitches with hardstanding and some are located at the perimeter fence overlooking the beach. Although sand based, the ground is firm and level. Roads are tarmac and there is direct access to the beach which is supervised by lifeguards. Occasionally a traditional music evening is organised on the site. Whilst a treat in store for visitors is the natural beauty of Achill, also worth seeing are Kildownet Castle, the Slievemore deserted village and the Seal Caves.

You might like to know

Achill is a haven for watersports enthusiasts, and keen golfers can play a round on the 9-hole course near the site.

☑ Beach on site
○ Beach within 1 km
☑ Sandy beach
☑ Blue Flag quality
☑ Lifeguard *(high season)*
○ Sun lounger and/or deckchair hire
☑ Watersports *(e.g. sailing or windsurfing)*
○ Snacks and drinks
○ Sunshades/sunbeds
☑ Dogs allowed *(on the beach)*

Facilities: The toilet block is spotless. Laundry room. Campers' kitchen including toaster, microwave and TV. Shop (June-Aug). Fresh milk and bread daily. Mobile homes for rent. Sun/TV room. Free WiFi over site. Courtesy bicycles. Off site: Walking, beach and fishing. Boat slipway 2.5 km. Pitch and putt 2 km. Riding 6 km. Pubs and restaurants. The JFK Arboretum, Johnstown Castle and Gardens, the Irish National Heritage Park, Kilmore Quay and Marina, and Curracloe beach (featured in the film Saving Private Ryan).

Open: Mid March - 31 October.

Directions: From the N25 south of Wexford town, outside village of Tagoat, follow signs for Lady's Island and Carne. After 3 km. pass Butler's Bar and take next left and continue for 2.5 km. Site is well signed.

GPS: 52.206433, -6.356417

Charges guide

Per unit incl. 2 persons and electricity € 20,00 - € 24,00	
extra person € 2,50	
child (2-16 yrs) € 1,50	

Ireland – Rosslare

Saint Margaret's Touring Park

Lady's Island, Rosslare Harbour (Co. Wexford)
t: 053 913 1169 e: info@campingstmargarets.ie
alanrogers.com/IR9170 www.campingstmargarets.ie

Accommodation: ☑ Pitch ☑ Mobile home/chalet ○ Hotel/B&B ○ Apartment

'This park is loved', was how a Swedish visitor described this family run, environmentally friendly caravan and camping park, the first the visitor meets near the Rosslare ferry port. Landscaping with flowering containers, maze-like sheltered camping areas and a pretty sanitary block all show the Traynor family's attention to detail. All 27 touring pitches have 6/10A electricity, are sheltered from the fresh sea breeze and ferries can be seen crossing the Irish sea. Just metres away, the safe, sandy beach (part of the Wexford coastal path) curves around in a horseshoe shape ending in a small pier and slipway. Tourist information on the area is provided in the well stocked shop. The immediate area boasts of thatched roof cottages and cottage gardens. The park is an ideal base from which to explore the sunny southeast or as an overnight stop to prepare for touring Ireland or for departure. Local lakes and the Saltee Islands, various locations of ornithological interest, deep sea and shore fishing, and award-winning pubs and restaurants provide something for everyone.

You might like to know

The safe sandy beach is on the Wexford Coastal path. Lady's Island and lake, the site of an ancient monastry, can be found along the coast. Also recommended are Kilmore Quay and Marina and Curracloe beach.

○ Beach on site
☑ Beach within 1 km
☑ Sandy beach
○ Blue Flag quality
○ Lifeguard *(high season)*
○ Sun lounger and/or deckchair hire
☑ Watersports *(e.g. sailing or windsurfing)*
○ Snacks and drinks
○ Sunshades/sunbeds
○ Dogs allowed *(on the beach)*

Facilities
Facilities: Three small blocks, plus facilities at the restaurant provide toilets, washbasins and free hot showers. Laundry service for a small fee. Campers' kitchens and sheltered eating area. Restaurant and takeaway (May-Oct). Pets are not permitted in rental accommodation or tents. Off site: Public transport from the gate during the summer months. Pub and shop 900 m. Riding 6 km. Golf 12 km. Boating, fishing and sea angling 200 m. Beach (pebble) 500 m.

Open: 1 April - 31 December.

Directions: From the N22, 17 km. east of Killarney, take the R569 south to Kenmare. In Kenmare take R571, Castletownbere road and site is 12 km.

GPS: 51.8279, -9.7356

Charges guide

Per unit incl. 2 persons and electricity € 21,50	
extra person € 4,00	
child (0-10 yrs) € 2,50	

Beara Camping The Peacock

Coornagillagh, Tuosist (Co. Kerry)
t: 064 668 4287   e: bearacamping@eircom.net
alanrogers.com/IR9580 www.bearacamping.com

Accommodation: ☑ Pitch ☑ Mobile home/chalet ○ Hotel/B&B ○ Apartment

Five minutes from Kenmare Bay, The Peacock is a unique location for campers who appreciate the natural world, where disturbance to nature is kept to a minimum. This five-acre site offers simple, clean and imaginative camping facilities. Located on the Ring of Beara, bordering the counties of Cork and Kerry, visitors will be treated with hospitality by a Dutch couple, Bert and Klaske van Bavel, almost more Irish than the Irish, who have made Ireland their home and run the site with their family. The variety of accommodation at Beara Camping includes caravan holiday homes, secluded hardstanding pitches with electricity and level grass areas for tenting. In addition, there are cabins sleeping two or four people and hiker huts sleeping two, ideal to avoid a damp night or to dry out. Bert and Klaske love to share with visitors the unspoiled natural terrain, its wildlife, the sheltered community campfire and advice on the walking and hiking routes in the area.

You might like to know

This site is situated on the beautiful Beara Peninsula, only 5 km. from Kenmare Bay. Here you will find marine and wildlife including seals.

- ○ Beach on site
- ☑ Beach within 1 km
- ○ Sandy beach
- ○ Blue Flag quality
- ○ Lifeguard *(high season)*
- ○ Sun lounger and/or deckchair hire
- ○ Watersports *(e.g. sailing or windsurfing)*
- ○ Snacks and drinks
- ○ Sunshades/sunbeds
- ○ Dogs allowed *(on the beach)*

Facilities: Seven modern, clean and well maintained toilet blocks include washbasins in cubicles, controllable showers and excellent facilities for families, young children and disabled visitors. Dishwashing and laundry rooms. Washing machines and dryers. Motorcaravan service point. Supermarket, bakery, restaurant, takeaway and café/bar (all w/e low season, otherwise daily). Swimming pools (heated and supervised) with slide, children's pool and pool games (9/5-15/9). Bicycle hire. Tennis. Extensive adventure playgrounds. Multisports court. Entertainment programme in July/Aug. WiFi throughout (charged). Off site: Fishing within 500 m. Nearest village is 2 km. Riding 3 km. Golf driving range 5 km.

Open: 22 March - 12 November.

Directions: Nieuwpoort is 19 km. southwest of Ostend. From east on A18 (E40) take exit 4 (Middelkerke). Turn north towards Diksmuide on D369; in 2 km. turn right on N367 towards Nieuwpoort. Pass through Sint-Joris and site is on the right.
GPS: 51.12965, 2.77222

Charges guide

Per unit incl. 4 persons
and electricity € 26,10 - € 38,00

dog € 2,80

Belgium – Nieuwpoort

Kompas Camping Nieuwpoort

Brugsesteenweg 49, B-8620 Nieuwpoort (West Flanders)
t: 058 236 037 e: nieuwpoort@kompascamping.be
alanrogers.com/BE0550 www.kompascamping.be

Accommodation: ☑ Pitch ☑ Mobile home/chalet ○ Hotel/B&B ○ Apartment

Near Ostend and convenient for the A18 motorway, this large, well equipped and well run site with 1,056 pitches caters particularly for families. There are many amenities including a heated pool complex, a range of sporting activities and a children's farm. The 469 touring pitches all have electricity (10A), 120 also have a water point and waste water drainage; they are in regular rows on flat grass in various parts of the site. With many seasonal units and caravan holiday homes, the site becomes full during Belgian holidays and in July and August. A network of footpaths links all areas of the site. Gates to the rear lead to a reservoir used for sailing, windsurfing and canoeing (canoes for hire) during certain hours only. Although the site is vast, there is a sense of spaciousness thanks to the broad stretch of landscaped leisure areas. These house sophisticated playgrounds, sports facilities and a children's farm. The site is well fenced, with a card-operated barrier and a night guard. Ostend is 19 km. away and offers activities and entertainment, while possible days out include Ypres and the First World War battlefields, Bruges and even Ghent.

You might like to know

Bicycles can be hired on the campsite and are a fun way to explore the seafront!

○ Beach on site
○ Beach within 1 km
☑ Sandy beach
○ Blue Flag quality
○ Lifeguard--*(high season)*
○ Sun lounger and/or deckchair hire
☑ Watersports *(e.g. sailing or windsurfing)*
○ Snacks and drinks
○ Sunshades/sunbeds
☑ Dogs allowed *(on the beach)*

Facilities: Three modern toilet blocks have good fittings, washbasins in cubicles (hot and cold water) and showers (€ 1.20). Baby bath. Facilities for disabled visitors. Laundry facilities with two washing machines and a dryer, irons and ironing boards. Motorcaravan service point. Shop. Snack bar and takeaway. Internet room (charged). Off site: Bicycle hire and sea with sandy beach 600 m. Riding 1 km. Golf 3 km. Boat launching 6 km. A bus for Bruges stops 200 m. from the site, a tram for the coast 400 m.

Open: 15 March - 15 October.

Directions: On E40/A10 in either direction take exit 6 for De Haan/Jabbeke. Follow N377 towards Haan-Bredene, at roundabout head towards Vlissegem. After 4 km. go straight on at junction. Turn right after a further 1.5 km. Site is 750 m. on right.

GPS: 51.28318, 3.05753

Charges guide

Per unit incl. 4 persons and electricity	€ 19,00 - € 28,00
extra person	€ 3,50
child (under 10 yrs)	€ 3,00
dog	€ 3,50

Belgium – De Haan

Camping Ter Duinen

Wenduinsesteenweg 143, B-8420 De Haan (West Flanders)
t: 050 413 593   e: info@campingterduinen.be
alanrogers.com/BE0578   www.campingterduinen.be

Accommodation: ☑ Pitch   ☑ Mobile home/chalet   ○ Hotel/B&B   ○ Apartment

Ter Duinen is a large, seaside holiday site with 120 touring pitches and over 700 privately owned static holiday caravans. The pitches are laid out in straight lines with tarmac access roads and the site has three immaculate toilet blocks. Other than a bar and a playing field, the site has little else to offer, but it is only a 600 m. walk to the sea and next door to the site is a large sports complex with a sub-tropical pool and several sporting facilities. Opportunities for riding and golf (18-hole course) are close by. It is possible to hire bicycles in the town. Access to the beach is via a good woodland footpath. There is a main road and tramway to cross, but there are designated pedestrian crossings. Cycling is very popular in this area and there are numerous good cycle paths, including one into the centre of De Haan (1.5 km). The best places to visit for a day trip are Ostend with the Atlantic Wall from WWII, Knokke (which holds many summer festivals) and Bruges.

You might like to know

The campsite is ideally situated for day trips to Bruges, Knokke and Ostend.

○ Beach on site
☑ Beach within 1 km
☑ Sandy beach
○ Blue Flag quality
○ Lifeguard *(high season)*
○ Sun lounger and/or deckchair hire
○ Watersports *(e.g. sailing or windsurfing)*
○ Snacks and drinks
○ Sunshades/sunbeds
○ Dogs allowed *(on the beach)*

Facilities:
The three sanitary blocks are modern and clean, with washbasins in cabins, a baby room and provision for visitors with disabilities. Laundry. Motorcaravan services. Supermarket with fresh bread daily, bar, restaurant, takeaway (all 1/4-31/10). Recreation room. Swimming pool complex. Play area. Only gas barbecues are permitted. Dogs are not accepted.
Off site: Riding 150 m. Beach and fishing 300 m. Golf 6 km. Katwijk within walking distance.

Open: All year.

Directions: Leave A44 at exit 8 (Leiden-Katwijk) to join N206 to Katwijk. Take Katwijk Noord exit and follow signs to site.

GPS: 52.21103, 4.40978

Charges guide

Per unit incl. 2 persons
and electricity € 23,50 - € 31,50

extra person € 4,00

Netherlands – Katwijk

Recreatiecentrum De Noordduinen

Campingweg 1, NL-2221 EW Katwijk aan Zee (Zuid-Holland)
t: 0714 025 295   e: info@noordduinen.nl
alanrogers.com/NL5680   www.noordduinen.nl

Accommodation: ☑ Pitch   ☑ Mobile home/chalet   ○ Hotel/B&B   ○ Apartment

This is a large, well managed site surrounded by dunes and sheltered partly by trees and shrubbery, which also separate the various camping areas. The 200 touring pitches are marked and numbered but not divided. All have electricity (10A) and 75 are fully serviced with electricity, water, drainage and TV connection. There are also seasonal pitches and mobile homes for rent. Entertainment is organised in high season for various age groups. A new complex with indoor and outdoor pools, restaurant, small theatre and recreation hall provides a good addition to the site's facilities. Seasonal pitches and mobile homes are placed mostly away from the touring areas and are unobtrusive. You are escorted to an allocated pitch and sited in a formal layout, with cars parked away from the pitches. However, with the super pitch your car can be parked on the pitch. Bicycles can be hired on site plus the nearby Space Expo is well worth a visit. The beaches are inviting and offer numerous possibilities for long walks and cycling tours.

You might like to know

The broad sandy beaches and sheltered dunes make this a beautiful area ideal for nature lovers, while being safe for young children.

○ Beach on site
☑ Beach within 1 km
☑ Sandy beach
○ Blue Flag quality
○ Lifeguard *(high season)*
○ Sun lounger and/or deckchair hire
○ Watersports *(e.g. sailing or windsurfing)*
○ Snacks and drinks
○ Sunshades/sunbeds
○ Dogs allowed *(on the beach)*

Facilities: Modern, first class sanitary building providing showers, washbasins, private cabins, family shower rooms and other facilities for children and disabled visitors. Launderette. Shop/mini market. Fresh bread (all year). Heated swimming pool. Play areas (indoors and outdoors). Sports field. Motorcaravan service point. Outdoor table football. Games room with Xbox stations. Small film theatre. Recreation room. Entertainment team (special holidays, weekends and July-Aug). Sauna. Whirlpool. First aid post. Free WiFi. Dogs welcome all year – showers available near sanitary block. Off site: Riding 1 km. Fishing 5 km. Golf 7 km. Boat launching 8 km.

Open: All year (with most facilities).

Directions: From the A15 take exit 12 towards Middelburg. Follow the N57 through Ouddorp and then turn right on the N652. Immediately turn left for the N651 and follow to Noordwelle. Site is well signed.

GPS: 51.739062, 3.802369

Charges guide

Per unit incl. 2 persons, electricity, water and waste water € 20,00 - € 46,00	
extra person (over 2 yrs) € 5,75	
dog € 4,00	

No credit cards.

Netherlands – Renesse

Strandpark De Zeeuwse Kust

Helleweg 8, NL-4326 LJ Noordwelle/Renesse (Zeeland)
t: 0111 468 282   e: info@strandparkdezeeuwsekust.nl
alanrogers.com/NL6948   www.strandparkdezeeuwsekust.nl

Accommodation: ☑ Pitch ☑ Mobile home/chalet ○ Hotel/B&B ○ Apartment

Whether you want relaxation, something for the children, the seaside or activities, you will find all of these at De Zeeuwse Kust located just 250 m. from the sea with its beautiful sandy beach. The outstanding, hotel standard facilities contained within the centrally located building are in a class of their own, offering a haven whatever the weather. From the open plan kitchen, the oversized wooden stools, to the open fireplace, they are all first class. This site has 168 spacious and comfortable pitches, some with private sanitary provision. The modern sanitary unit is heated and includes facilities for children and disabled visitors. The recreation team organises several activities for children all year. A heated pool and large indoor play area add to the facilities offered at this site which is highly recommended. There are walks and horse riding through the dunes, and the sea offers opportunities for kite surfing, diving, windsurfing and sailing (tuition available). This site is on the island of Schouwen-Duivenland, with views of the dunes and open countryside.

You might like to know

Just 250 m. from a North Sea beach. Visitors are welcome all year round!

○ Beach on site
☑ Beach within 1 km
☑ Sandy beach
☑ Blue Flag quality
○ Lifeguard *(high season)*
○ Sun lounger and/or deckchair hire
☑ Watersports *(e.g. sailing or windsurfing)*
☑ Snacks and drinks
○ Sunshades/sunbeds
☑ Dogs allowed *(on the beach)*

Facilities: One large and two smaller heated toilet blocks in traditional style provide separate toilets, showers and washing cabins. High standards of cleanliness, a dedicated unit for disabled campers and provision for babies. Warm water is free of charge. Dishwasher. Launderette. Motorcaravan services. Supermarket, snack bar, restaurant and takeaway (all season). Recreation room. Youth centre. Tennis. Playground and play field. Animal farm. Bicycle and children's pedal hire. Canoe, surf, pedal boat and boat hire. Fishing. WiFi over site (charged). Two cottages for hikers. No dogs allowed. Off site: Golf 3 km. Riding 6 km. Beach 7 km.

Open: 28 March - 30 September.

Directions: From the Amsterdam direction take the A4 (Europoort), then the A15 (Europoort). Take exit for Brielle on N57 and, just before Brielle, site is signed.

GPS: 51.9097, 4.18536

Charges guide

Per unit incl. 2 persons
and electricity € 18,00 - € 25,00

extra person € 3,30

child (under 12 yrs) € 2,80

Netherlands – Brielle

Camping De Krabbeplaat

Oude Veerdam 4, NL-3231 NC Brielle (Zuid-Holland)
t: 0181 412 363 e: info@krabbeplaat.nl
alanrogers.com/NL6980 www.krabbeplaat.nl

Accommodation: ☑ Pitch ☑ Mobile home/chalet ○ Hotel/B&B ○ Apartment

Camping De Krabbeplaat is a family run site situated near the ferry port in a wooded, recreation area next to the Brielse Meer lake. There are 448 spacious pitches, with 68 for touring units, all with electricity (10A), cable connections and a water supply nearby. A nature conservation plan exists to ensure the site fits into its natural environment. The lake and its beaches provide the perfect spot for watersports and relaxation and the site has its own harbour where you can moor your own boat. This excellent site is very convenient for the Europort ferry terminal. Plenty of cultural opportunities can be found in the historic towns of the area. Because of the large range of amenities and the tranquil nature of the site, De Krabbeplaat is perfect for families and couples.

You might like to know

The campsite is in a beautiful, wooded area next to the Brielse Meer lake, just a stone's throw from the sea. It borders on a region of extensive polders, pretty villages and historical towns.

☑ Beach on site
○ Beach within 1 km
☑ Sandy beach
○ Blue Flag quality
○ Lifeguard (high season)
○ Sun lounger and/or deckchair hire
☑ Watersports (e.g. sailing or windsurfing)
○ Snacks and drinks
○ Sunshades/sunbeds
○ Dogs allowed (on the beach)

Facilities: Sanitary building with heating, washbasins in cubicles and baby bath. Microwave. Dishwasher. Fresh bread. Cable television connection to all pitches. Motorcaravan service point. Animal corner. Sand pit. Jeu de boules area. Books, magazines and toys to borrow. Activity programme during holiday period (3 times a week). Trampoline. Telephone. WiFi throughout (charged). Dogs are not accepted. Off site: Restaurant opposite. Beach and fishing a few minutes walk over the sand dunes. Bus stop outside the entrance. Supermarket 50 m. Riding and bicycle hire 2 km.

Open: 28 March - 2 November.

Directions: Take the E312/A58 around the south of Middelburg then onto the N288 through Vlissingen and Zoutelande, after which the site is just over 1 km. on left.

GPS: 51.51046, 3.466318

Charges guide

Per unit incl. 2 persons
and electricity € 15,80 - € 28,50

Netherlands – Zoutelande

Camping Janse

Westkapelseweg 59, NL-4374 ND Zoutelande (Zeeland)
t: 0118 561 359 e: info@campingjanse.nl
alanrogers.com/NL7076 www.campingjanse.nl

Accommodation: ☑ Pitch ☑ Mobile home/chalet ○ Hotel/B&B ○ Apartment

Camping Janse is in the far southwest of Zeeland. It is a family, seaside site on the edge of sand dunes with the beach directly behind. There are 136 touring pitches, all 95 sq.m. with 6A electricity and water nearby, plus bungalows and caravans to rent. Some motorcaravan pitches are partly paved, and a field area (without electricity) is set aside for young people with small tents. Daily fresh bread is available and for other provisions the supermarket is 50 m. A restaurant with a terrace and play area for children is directly opposite the campsite entrance. In addition to the attraction of the sea and beach, there are opportunities for sports and activities on the site, and during the holiday period an organised activity programme runs three times a week. The site is on a cycle route and nearby there are walking and roller skating paths. Middelburg (13 km), the capital of Zeeland, has an historic centre and historic Veere (18 km) is a starting point for cruises on Lake Veere. The maritime city of Flushing is also well worth a visit.

You might like to know

This family site is just 2 km. away from the village of Zoutelande, and at the foot of the sand dunes.

- ☑ Beach on site
- ○ Beach within 1 km
- ☑ Sandy beach
- ○ Blue Flag quality
- ○ Lifeguard *(high season)*
- ○ Sun lounger and/or deckchair hire
- ○ Watersports *(e.g. sailing or windsurfing)*
- ○ Snacks and drinks
- ○ Sunshades/sunbeds
- ○ Dogs allowed *(on the beach)*

Facilities
Facilities: Heated sanitary blocks (cleaning variable) provide free showers. Child-size toilets and showers. Baby rooms. Facilities for disabled visitors. Laundry facilities. Motorcaravan service points. Shop. Bar, restaurant and snack bar. Open-air stage and soundproofed disco. Health/cure centre, solarium and sauna. Archery. Watersports. Minigolf. Internet café. Beach fishing. Riding. WiFi (charged). Off site: Boat launching 6 km. Golf 16 km.

Open: 1 April - 26 October.

Directions: After crossing the bridge follow road to Landkirchen and Petersdorf. From Petersdorf site is signed. It is 4 km. northwest of the town.

GPS: 54.48761, 11.0186

Charges guide

Per unit incl. 2 persons and electricity	€ 18,00 - € 35,30
child (under 17 yrs)	€ 2,00 - € 6,30
extra person	€ 4,00 - € 7,40

No credit cards.

Germany – Fehmarn

Strandcamping Wallnau

Wallnau 1, D-23769 Fehmarn (Schleswig-Holstein)
t: 043 729 456 e: wallnau@strandcamping.de
alanrogers.com/DE30070 www.strandcamping.de

Accommodation: ☑ Pitch ☑ Mobile home/chalet ○ Hotel/B&B ○ Apartment

With direct beach access and protected from the wind by a dyke, this family site is on Germany's second largest island (since 1963 joined to the Baltic sea coast by a bridge). This is a quiet location on the western part of Fehmarn Island in close proximity to a large bird sanctuary. Of the 800 pitches, 400 are for touring, all with electricity (6-16A) and on level grass areas arranged in alleys and separated by hedges. The island is low lying, ideal for leisurely walking and cycling, especially along the track that runs along the top of the dyke. The beach is a mixture of sand and pebbles, and in summer lifeguards are on duty. The southern part is a naturist area. For those with an ornithological interest, the bird sanctuary with over 80 species is worth visiting. Swimming, sailing and diving are possible in the sea and there is a windsurfing school. For those who prefer dry land there is pony riding for children and a riding school. During summer there are entertainment programmes for children and courses for adults; twice a week there are film shows.

You might like to know

The site boasts a specialist kite- and windsurfing school, its own dive centre and riding stables. Additionally, the site is located next to the Wallnau bird sanctuary.

- ☑ Beach on site
- ○ Beach within 1 km
- ○ Sandy beach
- ○ Blue Flag quality
- ☑ Lifeguard *(high season)*
- ○ Sun lounger and/or deckchair hire
- ☑ Watersports *(e.g. sailing or windsurfing)*
- ○ Snacks and drinks
- ○ Sunshades/sunbeds
- ○ Dogs allowed *(on the beach)*

Ostsee Camping

Strandstrasse 19c, D-23968 Zierow (Mecklenburg-West Pomerania)
t: 038 428 638 20   e: ostseecampingzierow@t-online.de
alanrogers.com/DE25000   www.ostsee-camping.de

Accommodation: ☑ Pitch   ☑ Mobile home/chalet   ○ Hotel/B&B   ☑ Apartment

Set on top of sand dunes overlooking and with direct access to the beach, Ostsee Camping is in a quiet location yet within easy reach of major towns in the region. There is good swimming from the beach, although the site does have a small swimming pool. Of the 486 level pitches, 321 are for touring units, all have electricity connections (10-16A) and 120 are fully serviced. They are set on grass and in places there is some tree shade. Outside of the site there are eight quickstop facilities with electricity connections. This is a good site for families, with entertainment in summer, playgrounds and a wide, gently shelving, sandy beach. This part of Germany, formally the DDR, is not that well known to tourists, yet it has a great deal to offer in the way of sandy beaches, attractive landscapes and historic towns, cities and buildings. Anyone travelling to the Baltic coast should make a point of passing through and allowing a few hours to visit Schwerin with The Schloss and its gardens set on an island in the Schweriner lake, the second largest in Northern Germany.

You might like to know

This all-year, family campsite is situated directly on the Baltic coast, between the old Hanseatic cities of Lübeck and Wismar.

☑ Beach on site
○ Beach within 1 km
☑ Sandy beach
○ Blue Flag quality
☑ Lifeguard *(high season)*
○ Sun lounger and/or deckchair hire
☑ Watersports *(e.g. sailing or windsurfing)*
☑ Snacks and drinks
○ Sunshades/sunbeds
☑ Dogs allowed *(on the beach)*

Facilities: Two modern, attractive and well maintained sanitary blocks, one completely renovated in 2013, have a special children's area and a baby bath. Showers (on payment). Bathrooms to rent. Laundry room with washing machines and dryer. Shop (1/5-1/10). Bar. Restaurant. Takeaway. Indoor heated swimming pool. Sauna, massage and cosmetic studio. Bowling alley. Small zoo. Indoor playroom. Volleyball. Watersports centre with windsurfing, sailing and catamaran sailing. Go-kart and bicycle hire. WiFi over site and Internet in reception (charged). Off site: Riding 200 m. Golf 8 km. Schwerin Schloss, Wismar (can be reached by cycleway). Rostock and Lübeck.

Open: All year.

Directions: Site is on the coast 6 km. northwest of Wismar. Leave Autobahn 20 at exit 8 Wismar Mitte, then north to Gägelow north on minor road to Zierow.
GPS: 53.9347, 11.3718

Charges guide

Per unit incl. 2 persons and electricity	€ 20,30 - € 29,70
extra person	€ 4,50 - € 5,70
child (5-14 yrs)	no charge - € 3,00
dog	€ 3,00

Facilities: Five superb toilet units include washbasins, roomy showers, spa baths, suites for disabled visitors, family bathrooms, kitchens and laundry facilities. Children's bathroom decorated with dinosaurs and Disney characters, and racing car baby baths. Motorcaravan services. Supermarket. Café/restaurant. TV rooms. Pool complex, solarium and sauna. Wellness facility. Western-themed indoor play hall. Play areas. Supervised play rooms (09.00-16.00 daily). Barbecue areas. Minigolf. Riding (Western style). Fishing. Dog showers. ATM machine. Off site: Legoland 70 km.

Open: 18 March - 23 October.

Directions: From Varde take roads 181/431 to Blåvand. Site is signed left on entering the town.

GPS: 55.54600, 8.13507

Charges guide

Per unit incl. 2 persons and electricity € 33,80 - € 61,80	
extra person € 10,90	
child (0-11 yrs) € 8,10	
dog € 4,00	

Denmark – Blavand

Hvidbjerg Strand Camping

Hvidbjerg Strandvej 27, DK-6857 Blavand (Ribe)
t: 75 27 90 40 e: info@hvidbjerg.dk
alanrogers.com/DK2010 www.hvidbjerg.dk

Accommodation: ☑ Pitch ☑ Mobile home/chalet ○ Hotel/B&B ○ Apartment

A family owned TopCamp holiday site, Hvidbjerg Strand is on the west coast near Blåvands Huk, 43 km. from Esbjerg. It is a high quality, seaside site with a wide range of amenities including a large wellness facility. Most of the 570 pitches have electricity (6/10A) and the 130 'comfort' pitches also have water, drainage and satellite TV. To the rear of the site, 70 new, fully serviced pitches have been developed, some up to 250 sq.m. and 44 with private sanitary facilities. Most pitches are individual and divided by hedges, in rows on flat sandy grass, with areas also divided by small trees and hedges. On-site leisure facilities include an indoor suite of supervised playrooms designed for all ages, with Lego, computers, video games, TV, etc. and an impressive, tropical-style indoor pool complex. This includes stalactite caves and a 70 m. water chute, the 'black hole' with sounds and lights, plus water slides, spa baths, Turkish bath and a sauna. A Blue Flag beach and windsurfing school are adjacent to the site and the town offers a full activity programme during high season. A member of Leading Campings group.

You might like to know

The special conditions here are due to the reef known as Horns Reef, which stretches 40 km. into the North Sea creating a lagoon on its south side.

☑ Beach on site
○ Beach within 1 km
☑ Sandy beach
☑ Blue Flag quality
○ Lifeguard *(high season)*
○ Sun lounger and/or deckchair hire
☑ Watersports *(e.g. sailing or windsurfing)*
○ Snacks and drinks
○ Sunshades/sunbeds
○ Dogs allowed *(on the beach)*

Denmark – Fjerritslev

Klim Strand Camping

Havvejen 167, Klim Strand, DK-9690 Fjerritslev (Nordjylland)
t: 98 22 53 40 e: ksc@klim-strand.dk
alanrogers.com/DK2170 www.klim-strand.dk

Accommodation: ☑ Pitch ☑ Mobile home/chalet ○ Hotel/B&B ○ Apartment

A large family holiday site right beside the sea, Klim Strand is a paradise for children. It is a privately owned TopCamp site with a full complement of quality facilities, including its own fire engine and trained staff. The site has 460 numbered touring pitches, all with electricity (10A), laid out in rows, many divided by trees and hedges, with shade in parts. Some 220 of these are extra large (180 sq.m) and fully serviced with electricity, water, drainage and TV hook-up. On-site activities include an outdoor water slide complex, an indoor pool, tennis courts and pony riding (all free). A wellness spa centre including a pirate-themed indoor play hall is a recent addition. For children there are numerous play areas, an adventure playground with aerial cable ride and a roller skating area. There is a kayak school and a large bouncy castle for toddlers. Live music and dancing are organised twice a week in high season. Suggested excursions include trips to offshore islands, visits to local potteries, a brewery museum and birdwatching on the Bygholm Vejle.

You might like to know

There is a bird reserve nearby and several inland lakes with fishing trips available.

- ☑ Beach on site
- ○ Beach within 1 km
- ☑ Sandy beach
- ☑ Blue Flag quality
- ○ Lifeguard *(high season)*
- ○ Sun lounger and/or deckchair hire
- ○ Watersports *(e.g. sailing or windsurfing)*
- ○ Snacks and drinks
- ○ Sunshades/sunbeds
- ○ Dogs allowed *(on the beach)*

Facilities: Two good, large, heated toilet blocks are central, with spacious showers and some washbasins in cubicles. Separate children's room. Baby rooms. Bathrooms for families (some charged) and disabled visitors. Laundry. Well equipped kitchens and barbecue areas. TV lounges. Motorcaravan services. Pizzeria. Supermarket, restaurant and bar (all season). Pool complex. Wellness centre with sauna, solariums, whirlpool bath, fitness room and indoor play hall. TV rental. Play areas. Crèche. Bicycle hire. Cabins to rent. WiFi over part of site (charged). Off site: Golf 10 km. Boat launching 25 km.

Open: 30 March - 21 October.

Directions: Turn off Thisted-Fjerritslev 11 road to Klim from where site is signed.
GPS: 57.133333, 9.166667

Charges guide

Per unit incl. 2 persons and electricity	€ 31,00 - € 50,30
extra person	€ 11,00
child (1-11 yrs)	€ 8,20

Facilities: Superb central toilet block includes washbasins in cubicles, controllable showers, family bathrooms (some with whirlpools and double showers), baby room and excellent facilities for disabled visitors. Excellent kitchen and laundry. Additional facilities to the far end of the site. Motorcaravan services. Supermarket. Restaurant. Takeaway. Indoor and outdoor swimming pools with flumes and slides. Solarium. Well equipped, fenced toddler play area and separate adventure playground. TV and games rooms. Internet café and WiFi. Barbecue area. Fishing. Minigolf. Off site: Beach adjacent. Bicycle hire and riding 10 km. Golf 12 km.

Open: 14 March - 20 October.

Directions: From Fåborg follow 8 road to Bøjden and site is on right 500 m. before ferry terminal (from Fynshav).

GPS: 55.105289, 10.107808

Charges guide

Per unit incl. 2 persons, 1 child and electricity DKK 225 - 385

extra child DKK 65

Credit cards accepted with 5% surcharge.

Denmark – Fåborg

Bøjden Strand Ferie Park

Bøjden Landevej 12, Bøjden, DK-5600 Fåborg (Fyn)
t: 63 60 63 60   e: info@bojden.dk
alanrogers.com/DK2200   www.bojden.dk

Accommodation: ☑ Pitch   ☑ Mobile home/chalet   ○ Hotel/B&B   ○ Apartment

Bøjden is located in one of the most beautiful corners of southwest Fyn (Funen in English), known as the Garden of Denmark, and may well be considered one of the most complete campsites in the country. With just a hedge separating it from the beach, it is suitable for an entire holiday, while remaining a very good centre for excursions. Arranged in rows on mainly level, grassy terraces and divided into groups by hedges and some trees, many pitches have sea views as the site slopes gently down from the road. The 295 pitches (210 for touring) all have electricity (10A) and include 65 new, fully serviced pitches (water, drainage and TV aerial point). Four special motorcaravan pitches also have water and waste points. There are indoor and outdoor pools, the latter with a paddling pool and sun terrace open during suitable weather conditions. Everyone will enjoy the beach (Blue Flag) for swimming, boating and watersports. The water is too shallow for shore fishing but boat trips can be arranged.

You might like to know

The campsite has its own kayak school, a modern indoor and outdoor pool complex and is convenient for day trips to Faaborg, a wonderful old seaport.

☑ Beach on site
○ Beach within 1 km
○ Sandy beach
☑ Blue Flag quality
○ Lifeguard *(high season)*
○ Sun lounger and/or deckchair hire
☑ Watersports *(e.g. sailing or windsurfing)*
○ Snacks and drinks
○ Sunshades/sunbeds
○ Dogs allowed *(on the beach)*

TopCamp Feddet

Feddet 12, DK-4640 Faxe (Sjælland)
t: 56 72 52 06 e: info@feddetcamping.dk
alanrogers.com/DK2255 www.feddetcamping.dk

Accommodation: ☑ Pitch ☑ Mobile home/chalet ○ Hotel/B&B ○ Apartment

Facilities: Both sanitary buildings are equipped to high standards. Family bathrooms (with twin showers), complete suites for children and babies. Facilities for disabled visitors. Laundry. Kitchens, dining room and TV lounge. Excellent motorcaravan service point. Well stocked licensed shop. Licensed bistro and takeaway (1/5-20/10; weekends only outside peak season). Large, indoor swimming pool and paddling pool (charged). Minigolf. Games room. Indoor playroom and several playgrounds. Event camp for children. Pet zoo. Massage. Watersports. Fishing. WiFi. Off site: Abseiling and pool. Amusement park.

Open: All year.

Directions: From south on E47/55 take exit 38 towards Præsto. Turn north on 209 road towards Faxe and from Vindbyholt follow site signs. From the north on E47/55 take exit 37 east towards Faxe. Just before Faxe turn south on 209 road and from Vindbyholt, site signs.

GPS: 55.17497, 12.10203

Charges guide

Per unit incl. 2 persons and electricity	DKK 265 - 340
extra person	DKK 75
child (0-11 yrs)	DKK 55
dog	DKK 20

This interesting, spacious site with ecological principles is located on the Baltic coast. It has a fine, white, sandy beach (Blue Flag) which runs the full length of one side, with the Præsto fjord on the opposite side of the peninsula. There are 413 pitches for touring units, generally on sandy grass, with mature pine trees giving adequate shade. All have 10A electricity and 20 are fully serviced. The sanitary buildings have been specially designed, clad with larch panels from sustainable local trees and insulated with flax mats. They have natural ventilation, controlled by sensors for heat, humidity and smell. Shaped blades on the roof increase ventilation on windy days. Heating, by a wood chip furnace (backed up by a rapeseed oil furnace), is CO_2 neutral and replaces 40,000 litres of heating oil annually. Rainwater is used for toilet flushing, but showers and basins are supplied from the normal mains, and urinals are water free. Water saving taps have an automatic turn off, and lighting is by low wattage bulbs with PIR switching. Recycling is very important here, with separate bins for glass, metal, paper, cardboard and batteries.

You might like to know

For something completely different, why not try your hand at abseiling?

☑ Beach on site
○ Beach within 1 km
☑ Sandy beach
☑ Blue Flag quality
○ Lifeguard *(high season)*
○ Sun lounger and/or deckchair hire
○ Watersports *(e.g. sailing or windsurfing)*
○ Snacks and drinks
○ Sunshades/sunbeds
○ Dogs allowed *(on the beach)*

Sweden – Torekov

First Camp Båstad-Torekov

Flymossa Vagen 5, S-260 93 Torekov (Skåne Län)
t: 043 136 4525 e: torekov@firstcamp.se
alanrogers.com/SW2640 www.firstcamp.se

Accommodation: ☑ Pitch ☑ Mobile home/chalet ○ Hotel/B&B ○ Apartment

Part of the First Camp chain, this site is 500 m. from the fishing village of Torekov, 14 km. west of the home of the Swedish tennis WCT Open at Båstad, on the stretch of coastline between Malmö and Göteborg. Useful en route from the most southerly ports, it is a well situated site and worthy of a longer stay for relaxation. It has 535 large pitches (390 for touring units), all numbered and marked, mainly in attractive natural woodland, with some on more open ground close to the shore. Of these, 300 have electricity (10A) and cable TV, 77 also having water and drainage. The modern reception complex is also home to a good shop, a snack bar, restaurant, and pizzeria. The spacious site covers quite a large area and there is a cycle track along the shore to the bathing beach. Games for children are organised in high season.

You might like to know

At nearby Torekov, fishing boats are available to hire. Alternatively, take a short boat ride to Halland Vadero for a seal safari or to swim in the safe, shallow water.

☑ Beach on site
○ Beach within 1 km
☑ Sandy beach
○ Blue Flag quality
○ Lifeguard *(high season)*
○ Sun lounger and/or deckchair hire
☑ Watersports *(e.g. sailing or windsurfing)*
○ Snacks and drinks
○ Sunshades/sunbeds
○ Dogs allowed *(on the beach)*

Facilities: Three good sanitary blocks with facilities for babies and disabled visitors. Laundry. Cooking facilities. Motorcaravan service point. Bar. Restaurant, pizzeria and snack bar with takeaway (21/6-4/8). Shop and kiosk (1/6-25/8). Minigolf. Play areas and adventure park for children. Boules and outdoor chess. Bicycle and go-kart hire. TV room. Beach. Fishing. WiFi over site (charged). Off site: Games, music and entertainment in high season. Tennis close by. Golf 1 km. Riding 3 km.

Open: All year (all amenities 20 June - 5 August).

Directions: From E6 Malmö-Göteborg road take Torekov/Båstad exit and follow signs for 20 km. towards Torekov. Site is signed 1 km. before village on right.

GPS: 56.43097, 12.64055

Charges guide

Per unit incl. 4 persons
and electricity SEK 190 - 305

Facilities: Three heated sanitary blocks provide a good supply of roomy shower cubicles, washbasins, some washbasin/WC suites and WCs. Facilities for babies and disabled visitors. Well equipped laundry room. Good kitchen with cookers, microwaves and dishwasher (free), and sinks. Hot water is free. Gas supplies. Motorcaravan services. Shop (1/5-30/8). Pizzeria, licensed restaurant and café (all 1/5-30/8). Bar (1/7-31/7). Outdoor heated swimming pool (15/5-22/8). Playgrounds. Bouncy castle. Boules. Canoe hire. Bicycle hire. Minigolf. Family entertainment and activities. Football. Off site: Golf 500 m. Riding 2 km. Fishing 4 km.

Open: 12 April - 30 September.

Directions: Cross Öland road bridge from Kalmar on road no. 137. Take exit for Öland Djurpark/Saxnäs, then follow campsite signs. Site is just north of the end of the bridge.

GPS: 56.68727, 16.48182

Charges guide

Per unit incl. electricity SEK 175 - 430

Weekend and weekly rates available.

Sweden – Färjestaden

Krono Camping Saxnäs

S-386 95 Färjestaden (Kalmar Län)
t: 048 535 700   e: info@kcsaxnas.se
alanrogers.com/SW2680   www.kcsaxnas.se

Accommodation: ☑ Pitch   ☑ Mobile home/chalet   ○ Hotel/B&B   ○ Apartment

Well placed for touring Sweden's Riviera and the fascinating and beautiful island of Öland, this family run site, part of the Krono group, has 420 marked and numbered touring pitches. Arranged in rows on open, well kept grassland dotted with a few trees, all have electricity (10/16A), 320 have TV connections and 112 also have water. An unmarked area without electricity can accommodate around 60 tents. The site has about 130 long stay units and cabins for rent. The sandy beach slopes very gently and is safe for children. Reception is efficient and friendly with good English spoken. In 2009 an outdoor heated pool and a children's pool were built at the entrance to the site. In high season children's games are organised and dances are held twice weekly, with other activities on other evenings. Nearby attractions include the 7 km. long Öland road bridge and the 400 old windmills on the island (in the 19th century there were 2,000). The southern tip of Öland, Ottenby, is a paradise for birdwatchers.

You might like to know

The gently sloping beach is safe for children and is cleaned daily. Youngsters will enjoy the Öland Animal and Amusement Park, just 3 km. away.

- ☑ Beach on site
- ○ Beach within 1 km
- ☑ Sandy beach
- ☑ Blue Flag quality
- ○ Lifeguard *(high season)*
- ○ Sun lounger and/or deckchair hire
- ○ Watersports *(e.g. sailing or windsurfing)*
- ○ Snacks and drinks
- ○ Sunshades/sunbeds
- ○ Dogs allowed *(on the beach)*

Facilities: Seven heated sanitary blocks provide a good supply of roomy shower cubicles, washbasins, some washbasin suites and WCs. Facilities for babies and disabled visitors (key at reception). Well equipped laundry rooms. Excellent kitchens with cookers, ovens, microwaves, dishwashers (free) and sinks. Motorcaravan services. Supermarket and bakery. Pizzeria, café, pub and restaurant. Takeaway. Bicycle hire, pedal cars and pedal boat hire. Minigolf. 9-hole golf course. Indoor/outdoor swimming pool (on the beach). Trim trails. Family entertainment and activities. WiFi. Off site: Fishing 4 km.

Open: 1 May - 1 September.

Directions: From Kalmar cross Öland road bridge on road no. 137. On Öland follow road no. 136 towards Borgholm and Byxelkrok. Turn left at roundabout north of Böda and follow campsite signs to Krono camping Böda Sand.

GPS: 57.27436, 17.04851

Charges guide

Per pitch SEK 155 - 285

incl. electricity SEK 245 - 395

Sweden – Byxelkrok

Krono Camping Böda Sand

S-38773 Byxelkrok (Kalmar Län)
t: 048 522 200 e: info@bodasand.se
alanrogers.com/SW2690 www.bodasand.se

Accommodation: ☑ Pitch ☑ Mobile home/chalet ◯ Hotel/B&B ☑ Apartment

Krono Camping Böda Sand is beautifully situated at the northern end of the island of Öland and is one of Sweden's largest and most modern campsites. Most of the 1,200 pitches have electricity (10/16A) and TV connections, 130 have water and waste water drainage. The pitches and 165 cabins for rent are spread out in a pine forest, very close to a fabulous 10 km. long, white sand beach. Here you will also find a restaurant, kiosks, toilets and beach showers, and a relaxation centre with an indoor/outdoor pool. The reception, the toilet blocks and the services at this site are excellent and comprehensive. Entertainment and activities both for children and adults are very extensive – there are more than 90 different items to choose from every week during high season. For exercise, there are tennis and badminton courts, trim trails, a football pitch and a nine-hole golf course (par 58) in the forest. Nearby attractions are the lighthouse at the northern tip of Öland, the Troll forest and the natural limestone sculptures at Byerum.

You might like to know

The white sand beach is cleaned daily.

☑ Beach on site
◯ Beach within 1 km
☑ Sandy beach
◯ Blue Flag quality
◯ Lifeguard (high season)
◯ Sun lounger and/or deckchair hire
☑ Watersports (e.g. sailing or windsurfing)
☑ Snacks and drinks
◯ Sunshades/sunbeds
◯ Dogs allowed (on the beach)

Facilities: The modern shower/WC blocks also provide male and female saunas, kitchen and launderette facilities. Facilities for disabled visitors. Motorcaravan service point. Playground. Reception with café/restaurant (June-Aug), souvenir and grocery shop. TV room. Free WiFi over site. Bicycle hire. Communal barbecues only. Off site: The adjacent Eden Centre provides excellent modern spa facilities where you can enjoy a day under the glass-roofed pool with its jacuzzis, saunas, Turkish baths and an Irish bath. Riding 2 km. Fishing 5 km. Golf 15 km.

Open: All year.

Directions: Leave road 4/E75 at junction with road 20 and head west down Kiertotie. Site well signed, Nallikari Eden, but continue on, just after traffic lights, cross a bridge and take the second on the right. Just before the Eden Centre turn right towards Leiritie and reception.

GPS: 65.02973, 25.41793

Charges guide

Per unit incl. 2 persons € 13,00 - € 26,00	
extra person € 4,00	
child (under 15 yrs) € 2,00	
electricity € 4,50 - € 6,50	

Finland – Oulu

Nallikari Camping

Leiritie 10, FIN-90510 Oulu (Oulu)
t: 044 703 1353   e: nallikari.camping@ouka.fi
alanrogers.com/FI2970   www.nallikari.fi

Accommodation: ☑ Pitch   ☑ Mobile home/chalet   ○ Hotel/B&B   ○ Apartment

This is probably one of the best sites in Scandinavia, set in a recreational wooded area alongside a sandy beach on the banks of the Baltic Sea, with the added bonus of the adjacent Eden Spa complex. Nallikari provides 200 pitches, 176 with 16A electricity (seven also have water supply and drainage), plus an additional 78 cottages to rent, 28 of which are suitable for winter occupation. Oulu is a modern town, about 100 miles south of the Arctic Circle, that enjoys long, sunny and dry summer days. The Baltic, however, is frozen for many weeks in the winter and then the sun barely rises for two months. In early June the days are very long with the sun setting at about 23.30 and rising at 01.30! Nallikari, to the west of Oulu, is 3 km. along purpose-built cycle paths and the town has much to offer. Nordic walking, with or without roller blades, seems to be a recreational pastime for Finns of all ages! You might even be tempted to buy a pair of long, brightly-coloured walking sticks yourself! Oulu hosts events such as the Meri Oulu Festival in July and the Oulu Music Video Festival and forms the backdrop to the mind boggling air guitar world championships.

You might like to know

Activities on the beach include beach volleyball, and there are beach tennis courts nearby.

- ☑ Beach on site
- ○ Beach within 1 km
- ☑ Sandy beach
- ○ Blue Flag quality
- ○ Lifeguard *(high season)*
- ○ Sun lounger and/or deckchair hire
- ○ Watersports *(e.g. sailing or windsurfing)*
- ○ Snacks and drinks
- ○ Sunshades/sunbeds
- ○ Dogs allowed *(on the beach)*

Been to any good campsites lately?

We have

You'll find them here...

The UK's market leading independent guides to the best campsites

... also here...

101 great campsites, ideal for your specific hobby,
pastime or passion

Want independent campsite reviews at your fingertips?

You'll find them here...

Over 3,000 in-depth campsite reviews at **www.alanrogers.com**

...and even here...

Want to book your holiday on one of Europe's top campsites?

We can do it for you. No problem.

The best campsites in the most popular regions - we'll take care of everything

alan rogers ⬤ travel

Discover the best campsites in Europe
with Alan Rogers

alanrogers.com
01580 214000

Index

Index

Index